DIARY OF A **VIAGRA** FIEND

DIARY OF A
VIAGRA
FIEND

JAYSON GALLAWAY

ATRIA BOOKS

New York • London • Toronto • Sydney

ATRIA BOOKS

1230 Avenue of the Americas
New York, NY 10020

ISBN: 0-7434-7080-X
      0-7434-7890-8 (Pbk)

First Atria Books trade paperback edition June 2005

10 9 8 7 6 5 4 3 2 1

ATRIA BOOKS is a trademark of Simon & Schuster, Inc.

Manufactured in the United States of America

For information regarding special discounts for bulk purchases,
please contact Simon & Schuster Special Sales at 1-800-456-6798
or business@simonandschuster.com.

Portions of the following chapters have appeared previously
(in various forms):

"Diary of a Viagra Fiend" on Salon.com, 1999
"A Spy in the House of Love" on GettingIt.com, 2000
"Dancer in the Dark" in *The San Jose Metro*, 2000
"The Art of Darkness" in *Just 18*, 2001

To my penis, without which none of this would have been possible, and even less of it worthwhile

Contents

Legal, Moral, and Ethical Disclaimer • **ix**

Diary of a Viagra Fiend • **1**

Hindsight on *20/20* • **12**

The Whore of the Ring • **49**

Burning Man—The Big BM • **90**

A Spy in the House of Love • **128**

The Great Italian Magazine Swindle • **140**

Dancer in the Dark • **166**

The Art of Darkness • **186**

Gossip Queen for a Day • **202**

I Come in Peace • **211**

Acknowledgments • **253**

Legal, Moral, and Ethical Disclaimer

This book is intended for mature audiences and not at all recommended for anyone under the age of 18. Both the author and the publisher of this work must insist that none of the self-destructive lifestyles or poor decisions or sordid situations in this work be imitated.

Most, if not all, of the names mentioned herein have been changed, but it was not to protect the innocent. Every one of these bastards is as guilty as a high-school senior with female footprints on the inside of his windshield the morning after prom night.

In addition to the warning appearing above, I must go further and insist that if you are pregnant, or of weak constitution, nervous disposition, or fragile psyche, be very careful.

If you are not a freethinker, or if you hide behind that lame euphemism of "political correctness," I must ask you to put this book down and politely fuck off. By all means, please, buy it. Please do. Buy two. Shit . . . send me a check directly. But do not read on. . . .

All right, listen, do whatever you want to do. I don't care. But do it with *passion*. And if your life lacks passion, meaning, depth, or self-determined purpose, and you are okay with that, well . . . I'll include you in my nightly prayers. But know that you could have achieved so much more if you had just not been so scared, so full of fear.

Okay, fuck it. If you've read this far, regardless of who you are, you may as well keep going. Maybe you'll laugh once or twice. Maybe you'll learn something. Or maybe you'll trade it in at a used bookstore for something involving Hobbits or golf. Regardless, I thank you for your kind attention thus far.

Take no shit.
Kick ass.
Mean it.
Don't ever, *ever* surrender.
And for God's sake, be *vital*.

For the Cause,
Jayson Gallaway

DIARY OF A **VIAGRA** FIEND

Diary of a Viagra Fiend

"Have you tried it?" he asks. I look up from my desk to find a middle-aged friend leaning toward me conspiratorially, his face an odd combination of deadly seriousness and abject glee. "Viagra . . . have you tried it?"

Christ.

Earlier today, I made a lame joke about Viagra. A coworker walking by snarked an offhand comment about the droopiness of a floral arrangement on my desk, and I jokingly suggested dropping a Viagra in the vase to "perk things up" a bit. I expected to hear a courtesy chuckle as he walked away, but I didn't. And now here he is, lurking ominously over me, essentially asking me if I have trouble getting it up.

"No!" I finally say defensively.

Why would I have tried it? That stuff is for old men whose spouses sleep in the spare room. I'm a virile, healthy, 29-year-old American male. Sure, there has been a time or two when, for reasons ranging from lack of interest to methamphetamine, little Tyson hadn't quite been ready to get in the ring when the bell rang. But that happens to everybody, right? Okay, yeah, so I recently acquired a 19-year-old girlfriend (let's call her "Lolita") and maybe I've been feeling just a tad insecure about not being capable of some of the erectile heroics I was capable of at 16, when random stiffies occurred more often than not, and were so solid they were almost prehensile: you could hang umbrellas on them (if you felt you *had* to).

But things are fine. . . . I haven't been worried about it.

"You should try it. Trust me," he says, "it's amazing."

But I . . .

"Doesn't matter . . . try it. You will thank me."

Hmmm. "Do you have any?"

"Nope. I just tried it last weekend. A buddy gave it to me. It's easy to get. Try the Net." He winks and walks away.

Hmmm.

Six hours later, I'm at home in front of the computer looking at one of about 47,000 Viagra Web sites I found and answering a confidential medical questionnaire over a secured Internet connection. Pretty basic stuff at first: name, date of birth, medicinal allergies. Then we get to the good stuff: No, I am not "experiencing erectile dysfunction" (really!), but for the sake of this experiment, I click the YES button. I hear a voice of dissent begin to growl from areas trousal. Soon it's crying out in rage at the slander that is being committed online. I tell it to calm down, that this is just an experiment, blah, blah, blah.

And then I realize I am speaking out loud to my penis. *Jesus, maybe I do have a problem.*

So I submit my form and my credit-card number, and am told that an online physician will carefully review my questionnaire, and, if his expert diagnosis determines that Viagra is right for me, my order will be shipped immediately via commercial carrier.

Two seconds after I click the OK button, I receive an e-mail saying the online physician has carefully reviewed my questionnaire (and presumably my credit-card number) and after much deliberation has decided that yes, Viagra is indeed for me.

Hot damn.

Twenty minutes later, the package arrives at my door. I rip open the package and find the holy pills complete with instructions. Highlights include the following:

- Take about one hour (preferably 90 minutes) before anticipated sexual activity with a snack or light meal. (Sexual activity with a snack or light meal? Is this stuff gonna make me want to mount a Twinkie?)
- Avoid fatty foods that can delay absorption.
- Stimulation is required for Viagra to work.
- Viagra should not be used more than once daily.

Is it just me, or would anybody else dating a spontaneous 19-year-old who is the keeper of very strange hours have trouble predicting whether or not they will be having sex an hour and a half from any particular moment? Though I am getting to know her pretty well, I have not yet learned to pinpoint her moods well enough to prognosticate the onset of uncontrollable libidinousness more than an hour before impact, let alone to maintain the mental wherewithal to then cavalierly ask for a snack or light meal low in fatty content.

And nowhere in the literature does it say how long the effects of the pills are supposed to last. So how crucial is the timing of this whole operation? What if, like many other drugs, when it wears off, you are left not just in the same shape you were before you took it, but worse? No conclusions. I pocket the bottle of pills.

It's around ten the next night and I'm sitting in an all-night diner with Lolita. As she quickly and predictably orders fried mozzarella sticks with Thousand Island dressing, I face a dilemma. I can't possibly order the Massive Fat Burger that is my usual fare: It is huge and fat, thus instantly violating two Viagratic prohibitions. But what am I going to do: Claim that I've suddenly started worrying about cholesterol and tryglyc-erides and order the skinless chicken patty with the little "Healthy Heart" icon next to it on the menu? I don't want to raise suspicions. Screw it . . . I order the Massive Fat Burger, the MegaFries, and a Big-Ass Shake. Fat content be damned.

As we eat dinner in relative quiet, my thoughts take on the form of a sixth-grade word problem:

Jayson and Lolita typically commence foreplay almost as soon as they climb into bed at night, and things proceed quickly from there, with intercourse beginning, on average, 13 minutes later. The white-trash diner they are presently sitting in is approximately 11 minutes away by car from Lolita's house. The Happy Pills in Jayson's pocket take approximately one hour to kick in when taken as directed. However, Jayson is railing against medical science by ingesting the better part of a cow and an inordinate number of MegaFries before taking the pills. Jayson can probably get Lolita to go to bed an hour after they arrive home tonight after dinner. Maybe an hour and a half. Assuming that it would be much better for the pill to kick in too soon (i.e., while brushing teeth) as opposed to too late (i.e., after Lolita has already entered REM sleep and has become less than receptive to any elephantine sexual overtures in the mid-dle of the night), then just when, pray tell, should Jayson take the frickin' pill?

Actually, if sixth-grade word problems had been like that, I probably would have done better in math.

I excuse myself and head for the can. In the stall, I open the container and shake one of the blue diamonds out onto my palm. I pop it. Then I pop another one. Just in case. You know the old drug-culture wisdom: "If yer gonna take one, ya might as well take two." Here we go.

On the way home, Lolita announces that we have to stop for gas.

"No! We can't!"

Shit. Did I actually just say that?

"What? Why not?"

"Uh . . . nothing . . . no. We can. I'm sorry. I just kinda wanta get home."

It's when she asks me if I'll "pump it" for her that it happens: Boner Time.

Jesus. It might just be a coincidence—it's only been 20 minutes (and I ate the Fat Burger). And since when does the idea of pumping gas qualify as "stimulation"? But this is not merely happenstance. This is a severe and random case of Hammer-cock the likes of which have not been seen in my pants since I was about 14.

We pull in to the gas station and for the first time in years I have a matter of seconds to figure out how best to hide a completely unsolicited Woody. Doing a weird little dance/hop thing as I get out of the car, I somehow manage to work it quickly into "high-noon" position, and am thus able to ambulate with relative normalcy and pump the gas.

I smile. Man, this is great. The surprise in my pants is like Elvis in the '68 comeback special, when he showed up all slimmed down, clad head to toe in black leather, looking like a bad ass, and everybody was damn glad to see he could still rock. Yeah. That's me. The voices from my crotch that were wailing and gnashing their teeth just 24 hours ago when I was ordering this stuff online are now cheering like college guys at their first wet t-shirt contest. There is much rejoicing throughout the pants.

Lolita is looking at me in the rearview mirror. She is giving me her "sexy" eyes. I think she senses something is up, as it were. I look at my watch: 27 minutes. I holster the gas pump and dance a sick little jig that involves several savage pelvic thrusts on my way to the passenger's seat.

"You're in an awfully good mood all of a sudden."

Well, darling, I think that's because if I were to stand facing due north, you could tell the exact time of night by the angle of the shadow cast in the moonlight by my gnomon. But all I actually say is, "Let's go home."

It's around 11:30 p.m. when we finally get back to her room. She begins looking through her formidable collection of CDs for something to listen to: a process that experience has demonstrated can take hours. I'm starting to worry that I'm going to peak (No pun intended. Actually, no pun achieved. Never mind.) here, only later to be left "hanging" when the time comes. I try to ignore the voices of doubt: The effects must last for hours, right? Let her choose a CD. I'll just lie languidly across her bed and try to exude my godlike state of arousal without being too obvious about it.

Thirty-seven minutes later, the appropriate CD has been selected and implemented. Soft music fills the room.

And now it is time for Love. I give her The Eyes and tell her to turn off the lights and Come Hither.

"No. I'm not tired yet."

I'm not tired either, woman. This ain't about tired. Git over here!

"And I need the lights on so I can read you some of what the kids wrote today."

Omigawd.

It is damn near midnight on a weeknight; we both have to be up early in the morning. Cockzilla is on the rampage in my drawers, and she wants to read me selections from essays written by the seven-year-olds she tutors. I wonder what would happen if I fed her one of these amazing blue diamonds.

About halfway through the 13th essay about something called Yu-gi-oh, it happens: deflation. In a way, I'm relieved. For an unrequited stiffie to go on for more than 90 minutes is kind of a spooky thing. There are worse problems to have, of course, but still, there can be too much of a good thing.

Finally, she finishes reading what must be about the 29th of these boner-killing kiddie rants, and I excuse myself to go to the bathroom to take out my contacts, etc. Lolita's an intelligent young woman: I'm sure she understands that this means "when I get back here, you'd better be buck-ass nekkid and ready for love."

If someone were to make a sci-fi/horror movie about my trip to the bathroom, it would have to star somebody large and hard and bald with a big hole in the top of his head who is always followed by two smaller, shadowy friends, and the movie will be called *Boner 2: Return of King Dong*. Or maybe *The ResErection: Back from the Dead*.

Yup. He's baaaaack.

Just walking into her bathroom, smelling the scent created

by all the girlie-girl products that are in the room: that's all it took. Once the contacts are out, I pelvic-thrust my way back down the hall to her room, where I'm quite sure I will find her in the prenominated state of buck-ass nekkidness.

No dice.

Lolita is sitting on the floor, Indian-style, fully clothed, playing solitaire.

"What are you doing?" I ask with more than a hint of menace.

"A tarot reading."

I climb into bed, doomed. My only hope is that she gets the all-too-elusive Boner Card.

I have found the key to heaven, but I cannot find the door.

I'm not sure how long I doze. Long enough to dream incredibly vivid dreams about various scenarios in strip clubs, girls' locker rooms, and a weird brothel in Peru in which I seem to have unlimited credit. I wake briefly. She is still on the floor, now painting her toenails. For what it's worth, it's been roughly two hours, and the General is still at attention.

I'd love to tell you about having the sort of carnal Olympics that fueled Prince's lyrics when he was cool; that we researched the entirety of the *Kama Sutra* and found it to be embarrassingly sophomoric; that the fleshly pleasures indulged that night would make Caligula blush. But it wouldn't be true. The awful truth is that I simply drifted off to sleep, alone, and dreamt of Carmen Electra.

I wake up in the morning feeling like I'm still dreaming. It feels like it's time to get up, but it is not the alarm clock that has awakened me: it is something much nicer than that.

It is her. Lolita!

She (evidently) finally came to bed, got a little sleep, and is now in the Mood. "Why now?" I wonder. Doesn't matter. What matters is that she is kissing my neck. But wait. What's this? I should be getting heroically aroused right now, but nothing's happening. I send several synaptic signals south. The only response I get is a tired little voice in my head that says, "Can't talk—coming down" and hangs up. Unbelievable.

Lolita is now chewing on my neck like it is a rawhide dog toy and I suspect she is in no mood to be refused. Having spent the entire previous evening in the state she is in now, I know all too well what she is going through. I panic.

"Wait . . ." I stop her. ". . . I hafta pee."

I grab my pants and canter down the hall. Lock the bathroom door behind me. Pee. Think. Okay. I run through the instructions in my head. A low-fat snack is simply out of the question. A one-hour, even a half-hour digestive period is unthinkable as well: We only have 20 disposable minutes until we're supposed to be commuting. Think. I look at myself in the mirror. The mirror . . . yeah. I pull the bottle of blue diamonds from my pocket and drop a pill onto a mirror lying on the counter. I use the plastic cap from the bottle to crush the pill and pull a credit card from my wallet to shape the powder into a line. A dollar bill quickly becomes a hollow cylinder and I lean over.

Viagra burns like nothing I've ever snorted in my life. For a moment, with the inside of my head on fire, I curse myself for being an idiot. And it's true: I am an idiot. But guess what? Two minutes later: Hi-yo Silver . . . I'm the Bone Ranger. Back down the hall, and for the next 16 minutes, a physical congress occurs that is indeed the stuff of legend. Enough said.

Thirty-seven minutes later I am on a commuter train, boner still intact, Viagra dripping down the back of my throat. I'm making horrible snorting noises and I smell like sex. Though the train is completely packed, no one sits next to me, which is fine, because I need some space to think. On the one hand, I am overjoyed at my new medical discovery and am thinking about having a big red-and-blue "S" tattooed on my you-know-what, maybe get it fitted for a little red cape. On the other hand, I have the new problem of trying to coordinate boner-pill intake with the hormonal swings of a girl who still wears Hello Kitty panties. *And I didn't have a problem in the first place!* Have I become instantly addicted to the Erection of the Gods?

I am going to be the charter member of a 12-step support group called VA: Viagraholics Anonymous.

I remember the hit of Ecstasy in my drawer at home. Normally, one hit of X is as useless as nonalcoholic beer. But in this case, it might be exactly what is called for. I call Lolita on her cell phone at school and tell her I've got a "surprise" for us. She says she is excited. Hah . . . she doesn't know the meaning of the word. I tell her to be at my place by 8:00 p.m.

People have asked me about that evening. My landlord has made several inquiries regarding the events of that night, in particular the felonious noise complaints and the damage to the ceiling fan over my bed (apparently those things are not made to rotate while supporting a naked woman: Hey, you live, you learn). My boss has questioned my absence from the office the following several days, and noted the bruises, scratches, and teeth marks that were visible even several weeks later. Yes, people have asked me about that night. All I tell them is that if the Olympics wanted real athletic competition, they would do away with that silly decathlon business and institute the Decatha-Hump, an event in which a male participant ingests a Viagra and is locked in a room with a girl who is crazy on Ecstasy. Whoever can still walk after 10 hours wins.

The details of that evening are so carnal, so profane, so unspeakably decadent, that I can't even think about them without becoming dangerously aroused. Of course, these days, now that I am eating Viagra pills like they are M&Ms, there is not much I can do without becoming aroused. As a matter of fact, I am actually typing this with my penis.

Suffice it to say this stuff works like a bastard. But if you don't really need it, don't even try it.

My bill at Temporarily Yours Escort Service is not something I can think about while sober, and my perpetually engorged member has scared even my cats into seeking more peaceful accommodations elsewhere.

But I guess there are worse problems a guy can have.

Hindsight on 20/20

"Mmmmhello?"

That's about the best I can do when I pick up a ringing phone before noon. It's damn near miraculous I can get even that out if the phone rings before 8:00 a.m.

Whenever the phone rings before 8:00 a.m., I know it means trouble. It means somebody wants something, and they want it now. Whether it's a relative in dire need of repayment of a loan, or some friend wanting bail money, those who call before 8:00 a.m. are inevitably needy. I am not a big fan of the needy, particularly when they have my phone number, and for years I have tried to shield myself from early-morning telephonic interlopers. For a while I turned the ringer off when I went to bed, letting voice mail handle the nonsense on the other end of the call. But with my parents getting older, and the increasing possibility that the person wanting bail money could very well be my date for a drug orgy later in the day, I have taken to leaving my ringer on throughout the night. I figure that if someone does actually corrupt my slumber by an inordinately early phone call, I shall give them the sort of emotionally damaging tongue-lashing that would induce dark Pavlovian breakdowns in even the most seasoned telemarketer. Which would be a fine strategy if I was ever awake enough at 8:00 a.m.

to do it. But I am not. I am in that unmirthful and sleepy purgatory between actual wakefulness and simple functionality on some weird reflex level just this side of dreamland.

And so it is now, when I growl out a barely interpretable, "Mmmmhello?"

Given my somniloquistic state, my recollection of this entire conversation is, at best, an educated guess based on the humiliating chain of events that unfolded over the next 48 hours or so.

Partial transcript of initial telephonic contact between Ted Lipshitz, producer for ABC's 20/20 and Jayson Gallaway, freelance writer who is trying to sleep.

Jayson: Mmmmhello?

Ted: Can I speak to Jayson Gallaway, please?

Jayson: Mmmyeah . . . thassme.

Ted: Hi, Jayson. This is Ted Lipshitz with ABC's *20/20*. How ya doing?

Jayson: Goddammit, Boochie, is that you? I'm not falling for any of your bullshit anymore. And fuck off . . . I'm trying to sleep. What the hell time is it anyway? Why aren't you asleep?

Ted: This isn't Boochie. This is Ted Lipshitz. I am a producer at ABC's *20/20*. And it's almost 11:00 a.m. here in New York City.

Jayson: Not Boochie?

Ted: Nope. Not Boochie. Ted Lipshitz. *20/20.*

Jayson [suddenly awake; stupidly]: You mean *the 20/20?*

Ted [chuckling patiently]: Yes, *the 20/20.*

Jayson: With Barbara Walters?

Ted: That's us.

Jayson: Holy shit.

Ted: Yes. Indeed.

Jayson [now alarmingly awake]: What can I do for you, Ted?

Ted: Well, we're doing a story about Viagra and its use with younger people in conjunction with other drugs, and in our research, we came across your story on *Salon.com*.

Jayson [to self]: Uh-oh.

Ted: Great stuff. Hilarious.

Jayson: Uh . . . thanks.

Ted: So like I was saying, the story we're doing is about younger people using Viagra, and *not* simply for erectile problems.

Jayson: Well, you came to the right guy, Ted. I do not have erectile problems. None at all.

Ted: Yes . . . that's what your story said, and that's a large reason we want to talk to you.

Jayson: It is large, isn't it, Ted?

Ted: What do you mean?

Jayson: Never mind. You were saying?

Ted: Well, one angle we're looking at is the use of Viagra in combination with other drugs. Like Ecstasy. Like in your story.

Jayson [even more awake, with a hint of malice]: Are you a law-enforcement agent, or in any way affiliated with law enforcement?

Ted: Not at all.

Jayson: And, you want to put me on TV?

Ted: We'd like to send a camera crew and one of our reporters to interview you for our show. Do you think you could be as candid in front of a camera as you were in your story?

Jayson: Wow. Um . . . hmmm. Well, I'm definitely interested. But, uh, I think I need a minute to think about it. I need
to wake up. Can I think about it and get back to you?

Ted: Well, here's the thing . . .

Jayson: There's a thing?

Ted: Well, we want to do this for a sort-of Valentine's Day
thing, so we'd like to shoot Friday. The day after tomorrow. So
we need a pretty quick decision.

Jayson: Can you give me 45 minutes?

Ted: Take an hour.

Once I had scrawled Ted's number down on my lamp
shade, I hung up the phone, looked bewildered, and said, out
loud, "Holy shit." I instantly began pacing circles around my
apartment. The press-whore part of me who had lain dormant
until this moment begins lobbying viciously for a "Yes" vote.
"You're a struggling and unknown writer drowning in debt and
poverty and complete despair and here's a national . . . no, an
international avatar of the Great God Television summoning
you to its perfumed and high-frequency electromagnetic analog
and digital waves, seeking your wisdom, wisdom so important
that this Great God will instantly, through its unquestionable
omnipresence and seeming omnipotence over all mankind,
share . . . no . . . *force* said wisdom into the conscious thought
of every commercially significant man, woman, and child who
compose ABC's formidable worldwide demographic."

But then, the more sensible side of me, the one that will
have to answer the phone when the Call comes from the parents (and you can bet your ass it will come) seconds after, or
worse, perhaps, *during* the broadcast of this segment, demand-

ing explanation, speaks up: "Shame! Shame on you for even considering appearing before an audience of millions of wholesome viewers and their sponge-minded issue and talking about your odious penis. And what about the drugs? Let's not forget about the drugs! You ass."

More pacing in circles. Cannot stop pacing. Call a few friends—four, to be exact. They are split evenly, of course. The ones who work in PR and medicine bemoan my lack of common sense and the inevitable doom that lack will bring like a Greek Chorus. The ones with defiantly unnatural hair colors who work in music and graphic design think that any hesitation is absurd, that I have no choice, that it is, like it or not, my job, and be sure to tell them when it will air.

I stop pacing only long enough to put on a pair of pants and a shirt, and then the circular peripatetic think session continues. My pacing on the hardwood floors infuriates the adipose Russian woman with the horrible toenails (who I once saw eat something she had just harvested from her own bulbous nose) in the apartment below, who is forever infuriated by this pacing and most any other sound coming from my apartment and who expresses her infuriation by doing exactly what she is doing right now, which is violently poking and jabbing her ceiling/my floor with what I'm guessing is a broom handle or a pool cue like some Slavic Ahab obsessively prodding the pacing White Whale above. She is interrupting my thought process at a very crucial point. This will not stand.

Because my ceilings are vaulted, I am able to get three progressively higher jumps on my mattress and box spring before landing squarely on the floor with substantial sonic impact that I'd estimate is the residential equivalent of a Daisy Cutter bomb. Not only does her ceiling-stabbing stop instantly, but I can hear the quite-audible fallout of trinkets and fixtures and communist artifacts that have been jolted from their assigned places and have followed gravity zealously to the floor below.

"Take that you booger-eating bitch! Quit prodding my thoughts with that fucking broom and go get a pedicure, ferchrissakes!"

My hour was almost up. In such moments of indecision with regard to matters of extreme, potentially life-changing importance, I defer to a simple question: "WWARD"—What Would Axl Rose Do?

Laugh if you'd like: I embrace and strongly endorse this method of reasoning. Even though I've never met Axl Rose, I somehow know exactly what he'd do in any given situation, and thus convoluted inner conflicts like the one above are solved in a second. Shit yes, Axl would talk cock on ABC during prime time. And he'd get good and drunk before the camera crew even got there.

I call New York and RSVP in the enthusiastically positive. Ted is thrilled, relieved even. I get the impression that he's had a tough time finding anyone stupid enough to go on network television and discuss the functionality of his sexual unit. I give him my address and other trivia, and Ted tells me the reporter will be calling to firm up (he laughs at his ironic play on words) plans for Friday.

Then, knowing I obviously have no clue of the magnitude of the mistake I've just agreed to, Ted gives me a quick primer on how such things work. A reporter, evidently a freelancer (not Barbara Walters), and a crew will come to my apartment Friday night, around 8:00 p.m., set up, and interview me about my penis and my drugs and how the two get along. Then, the reporter and crew will follow me around town ("You should bring a friend or two. Do you have any friends?"), filming me at hip bars and dramatically stylized nightclubs as I try to chat up potential holsters for my allegedly chemically engorged Love Gun. The footage obtained by the trailing around town of the camera crew is known in the television news business as "B-roll" and is what viewers will watch on screen while Barbara Walters or whatever anchor person does an expository and didactic VO (voice-over) regarding statistics and so on.

It isn't until we thank each other and hang up that it really hits me: Life as I know it is about to end. I wrote a hyperrealistic story about Viagra, and I'm about to replace Bob Dole as the poster boy for erectile dysfunction.

I am screwed.

I call Ted back. He has gone to lunch and is not expected back today. My call-waiting signal beeps. I click over. The voice on the other end is both female and pleasant. It is the freelance reporter who will be interviewing me, and I can tell by her barely detectable nervousness that she is about as enthusiastic about doing this interview as I now am. I think about backing out, but then I remember: WWARD? I can hear Axl talking to me, sending me strength and encouragement in his low, baritone speaking voice: "Go on, dude . . . rock out with your cock out." I give the reporter directions from Marin to my apartment on 8th and California, and we joke with each other about the patent absurdity of the situation, of the essential pretext of this "news" story. Her voice and demeanor relax me, and I think she is equally relieved to find that I'm not some drug-hoovering nymphomaniac who is going to immediately start dry-humping her leg as soon as she knocks on my door. In fact, I am sure this is what she is thinking because she tells me so.

"I'll wait until we're filming B-roll in some seedy nightclub and yank you onto the dance floor and frottage your thigh then," I reply. She titters nervously and hangs up, I suspect then making a beeline for the dictionary to look up "frottage." Somehow, I am suddenly at ease with the whole deal.

Once I hang up from her, I call Kristoffer, my only male friend, tell him the news, and instruct him that he must cancel whatever plans he may have had for Friday night and come over to my place, and imbibe robust and potent drink, and play the role of "my friend" as we go pick up girls at clubs whilst being trailed by an entourage of a reporter and a film crew. Oh yeah . . . and ABC is picking up the bar tab.

"What the fuck are you talking about?"

I retell him the whole story of the phone call, and of Ted and the pacing and Ahab the Commie and B-roll and yeah.

"Sounds like Boochie," he says.

"That's what I thought, but this guy is far more intelligent than Boochie could ever pretend to be. And I had to call the guy back in New York . . . the right area code, the whole bit. And some chick answered the phone, 'ABC?' I think it's the real deal."

Silence on the line for a few beats. Kristoffer exhales, demonstrative of deep thought.

"Hmmm. It doesn't have Boochie's hoof prints, but it smells like a prank. It has the stink of a setup. Have you made any enemies lately?"

I snicker.

"Yeah . . . duh . . . no need to answer that one. Tough call. There is the stench of a prank. Can you smell it?"

I sniff the air in the room. I smell the phone. Nothing.

"Nothing malodorous here," I say.

"Well, it's enough to gag a maggot where I'm sitting."

Then I hear a flush on his end of the line.

"I don't think that's prank you're smelling, my friend."

"I know the difference between shit and a carefully orchestrated prank. They are similar, yes, but one is far more potent than the other, and I am practically choking on the stench of prank here."

"Whatever. Just be here at seven on Friday night. And bring booze."

True to form, Kristoffer begins pounding on my door like a cop with a warrant at precisely 7:00 p.m., his motorcycle helmet in one hand, a bottle of cheap hooch in the other. He blocks my peephole with a gloved hand, so I make him wait an additional minute or so. Soon, he begins kicking the bottom of my door. The ruckus awakens the dormant communist with the horrible toenails downstairs and she begins to bellow. Big bellowing below.

I open the door, ignoring Kristoffer, and holler back: "Nyet!" And again, she is silenced. Kristoffer, who has learned during the weird years of our friendship to expect damn near anything, looks at me with a mixture of terror and pleasant curiosity. I can tell he wants an explanation.

"Never mind what they say on the news. The Cold War is most definitely *not* over. At least not here. Get inside, quick."

Convinced that this *20/20* business is all just an elaborate hoax, Kris approached the evening as simply another one of our cheap-booze-fueled, vandalism-and-petty-theft party nights, and he immediately cracked open his bottle of liquor in the kitchen and poured us each liberal shots of some thick viscous liquid. He handed me mine and I stared at it, holding it up to the light and grimacing.

"What's this shit floating in it? What the hell is this?"

"That 'shit' is gold . . . actual flakes of gold, and this fine beverage is cinnamon schnapps."

"You have *got* to be kidding me! I'm going on network television and I need to have a decent drink to relax and you bring me schnapps! With floaters in it?"

"Gold floaters, goddamnit. This stuff wasn't cheap. Now quit whining and drink."

"Am I supposed to drink the gold floaters?"

"Shit yes . . . that's the best part. That's like drinking the worm in the tequila. It'll make you hallucinate."

"You are *so* full of shit."

"Only about that last part. It doesn't make you hallucinate. But if we dispatch this whole bottle, gold floaters and all, by tomorrow night we'll be shitting Pac-Men."

It's unclear what he means, but I raise the glass to my lips. The stuff has the consistency of cough syrup and an equally pungent smell, the cinnamon odor failing to mask the brutal stench of the stuff in the same way that scented aerosol in a recently used bathroom only exacerbates an already-bad situation by making it smell like someone shit a Christmas tree. But still, I drink. After all, it's for the Cause.

"For the Cause," I say as I throw back a huge gulp of schnapps, as does Kris.

The second slug is much better than the first, and by the fifth belt of schnapps, I'm thinking that perhaps it's not an entirely bad thing. It is then that Kristoffer pulls out an incredibly fetid cigarette, without filter, poorly rolled, from the inside pocket of his leather jacket.

"We need to smoke this right away. I found it on the sidewalk outside your building. It is obviously a gift from the Fates, and you do not want to fuck with the Fates, particularly on a night like this."

True that.

Snatching up my lighter, he lights the thing and inhales deeply. He passes the joint to me, and somehow manages to speak without using any breath: "Don't ever fuck with Fate . . . for the Cause. Fuckin' A."

About halfway through both the bottle and the joint, while we were both sitting on my fire escape watching a girl in a neighboring apartment change clothes, Kris almost had me believing that I really had been set up by some mean-spirited former acquaintance. I was mentally coming to terms with this possibility when a knock came at the front door. The look of stunned surprise on my face was completely eclipsed by the disbelief and shock on his.

"Ha!" I exclaimed. "It's *real!*"

I felt victorious, but also completely drunk and, well, about as high as a giraffe's ass. I was in no mood to even deal with trying to open the door, much less speak On the Record to an audience of millions. I couldn't even bring to mind my middle name, and was concentrating deeply, trying to remember what my middle name was, when the knock came again, this time even harder.

"You'd better get that. It's your job," said Kris, calm as the Dalai Lama. Of course he was calm. ABC didn't give a rat's ass about interviewing him. He just had to sit back, decidedly *behind* the camera, drink his goddamn schnapps, and chuckle with dark mirth as he watched this for-broadcast debacle unfold.

At some point since Kris's arrival, I had become more paranoid than John Bobbitt at a cutlery convention.

"What if it's the police?" I thought, or said, or thought I thought but actually said because Kristoffer then answered: "I think that might be the lesser of two evils for you right now. Open the fucking door."

We carefully climbed back through my bathroom window and I yelled, "Coming!" at the door, and then, looking at Kristoffer who was still clad head to toe in his black leather riding gear and looking for all the world like the Gimp from *Pulp Fiction* without the mask with the zipper mouth and realizing the potential homoerotic implications of what I had just yelled at the door through a haze of pot smoke, I restated my position: "I'll be right there."

Great. They think we're hurriedly putting our clothes back on. This is bad.

Through the peephole I see a whole gaggle of people, none of whom appear to be law-enforcement agents or in any way affiliated with law enforcement.

I undo the five locks on the door (which, given my substantially altered state, is not too different from trying to artfully solve one of those fucking Rubik's cubes) and am greeted by three smiling faces, one male, two female. I say nothing. Hell . . . I'm still trying to remember my middle name. The female nearest me, the alpha female, speaks up.

"Jayson?"

I am still obsessed with remembering my middle name

when I reply, "No . . . that's my *first* name." They all suddenly
look as bewildered as I do.

"Oh . . . wait . . . no . . . yes . . . Jayson . . . yes . . . that is me.
I am him. I am he." I extend my hand and the alpha female
shakes it kindly. She introduces herself as the Reporter, the
male as the Camera Guy, and the other female as the Sound
Girl. I have already forgotten all three names and am again
working on my own middle name when it occurs to me to
invite them in, which I do.

They all pause to nervously eye Kristoffer, who has inexpli-
cably begun removing my various hunting knives and switch-
blades from their drawer, and is now polishing their blades
with creepily reverential care.

"Oh . . . that's Kristoffer, my only male friend. He is heterosexual, despite the fact that he is clad entirely in black leather. I
don't know why he is cleaning my knives. I don't use them
much. Say hello, Kristoffer."

Kris gently puts down the barbed gutting tool he is holding,
and is suddenly the model of politeness and charm. He introduces himself to the Reporter and crew, and even with a second
round of names, I forget all of them immediately. As this
occurs, I walk to my day planner on my desk and turn the page
to tomorrow, and under the blank "Things To Do" section, I
scrawl "Middle Name?" close the planner and try to forget the
whole thing.

Kristoffer is talking shop with the Sound Girl, who, he
quickly ascertains, turns out to be married to the Camera Guy,
who is himself wandering around my bed with some strange
and abstruse instrument held at arm's length from his face,
measuring an atmospheric aspect or some such. Because he

begins installing temporary dimmers on all of my light switches and lamps, I assume he has been measuring light levels. But I keep a suspicious eye on him nonetheless, even as the Reporter engages me in friendly, preinterview banter.

"Great apartment," she says nervously, looking around at the knives and the deflated, multiorificed, blow-up doll crumpled in the corner.

"Yes. Home shit home."

"It's better than anything I had when I lived in the City," she says.

"Me, too," chimes in the Camera Guy from under my bed, which Camera Guy I am beginning to suspect is a mole. Not a spy or a double agent, but an actual *mole,* a fuzzy little animal accustomed to the dark that burrows under things and feeds on worms and larva. Yes, I am admittedly as high as a kite. But this guy is tossing spent and empty lube tubes and my lucky condom from beneath the bed as he digs around for an electrical outlet or God knows what.

Kristoffer appears at my side with yet another generous cup of schnapps: "Drink this . . . it will straighten you out a bit . . . help you relax. You're too tense. Quit staring at the Camera Guy."

I take a belt of the thick cinnamon 80-proof syrup. "Doesn't he need a warrant to do that? He just threw my lucky rubber across the room!"

"You consented to search when you let them in . . . Fourth Amendment. Now drink your schnapps. Drink deeply from the waters of forgetfulness. It's the only thing that can help you now."

I'm sucking back schnapps in a tragicomic and doomed

attempt to become more drunk than stoned, somehow thinking that would be a more productive mind-set for an interview of this magnitude. The Reporter tries to keep the chitchat going: "I just *loved* your story," she says, pulling out a folded hard copy of the thing, which copy appears to have been through quite a bit of trauma. It is all dog-eared and many parts have been underlined. There are notes in the margins.

"Holy shit!" I think to myself (praying I don't say it out loud). I haven't read that thing since I wrote it and sent it to *Salon,* and that was a first draft. Now she's got it all *analyzed! Deconstructed. Fuck.* One mention of Derrida or Foucault and I will pounce. No good can come of this.

It takes the crew about half an hour to set everything up, and that time, combined with the once heinous but improving-with-every-sip schnapps is enough to settle my nerves and focus my mind enough to do what I'm told.

"Sit up straight . . . chin up," say voices from beyond the light. I'm sitting uncomfortably on the floor, leaning up against the foot of my bed in front of the camera as the crew tries placing different colored gels over their spotlights. That part is painless, but when they collectively gather around and look at my image on a monitor I can't see, trying to decide which color is best, I get a bit sensitive.

"Try dark blue. Or black. The darker it is, the better I look," I say with near papal ex cathedra. They look at me as though I've just proposed a circle jerk. But fuck them. *It's true: I am devastatingly handsome in absolute blackness.*

Some sort of consensus is reached with regard to the lighting, and the Reporter starts making with the banter again as the Sound Girl hangs a pendulous black phallic thing that looks like a Muppet's proboscis, if that Muppet had just been kicked in the beak by Snuffleupagus. As I continue to suck schnapps, I realize that it is a microphone on a telescoping stick. At first I suspect that she, along with everyone else in the room (including that bastard Kristoffer, who has logged online using my name and is chatting profanely with teens who have ages of dubious legality), is keeping her/their distance because my weed-and-schnapps breath stinks like a full sack of assholes. Which it does. Cinnamon ones, with bits of gold.

However, it is soon revealed that everyone is staying "out of frame," which I expected from the techs, and Kris (at least for the moment), but what about the Reporter? She was just another vague shadow *behind* the now-gelled lights and huge camera, which, by the way, is black and metal and has intimidating edges, and if you've never had an equally black and metal and edgy tripod pointed at you, you have no idea how actually aggressive and weaponlike and militaristic those things are. I instantly understand why celebrities so often get into brutal scuffles with the media: It's almost a defensive reflex. Add to this the effect of intensely focused spotlights and a disembodied voice coming from the darkness beyond, and it should be little wonder that I have the urge to confess to things I've never even done.

A fight almost erupts when the Camera Guy tries to take my glass of schnapps. A quick truce is brokered by his wife: I can keep my schnapps as long as I put it down in this one particular spot on the floor and don't drink it in the middle of answering a question. Fine.

But just as soon as that situation is defused, another one of equal potential danger arises.

"Hmmm . . . you are shiny," says the Reporter. And without

further explanation or justification pulls from her purse what I believe women refer to as a "compact," but what I know heterosexual men refer to as makeup. I know a few strippers who use such things to conceal their drug stashes, and when the Reporter says, "We need to powder your nose," my first thought is *hot damn!* I'm thinking she's going to bust out some sort of illegal powder, chop a couple of rails, and we're all gonna get our snort on. "All right!" I say, "You brought some sniff? That's just what we need to make this interview all it can be." Given the look she gives me, I may as well have just asked for some lubricant and directions to the nearest grade school. She opens the thing, dabs once or twice at it, and then just lunges at me with a well-powdered puff pad. My senses, already on a heightened state of alert, shift gears into the fight-or-flight level and I retreat brusquely from the advancing cosmetics. After some calming words of reassurance, I allow the Reporter to apply powder to my forehead, nose, and cheeks. When I think she has applied enough, I tell her that her soft touch is arousing me, and she stops immediately. She smiles. Good. She knows I am kidding but gets the point.

Last-minute tweaks and adjustments are made, and within moments we are "rolling."

It is worth noting here that I am by nature private to the point of what some people (many people, in fact) call "secretive." I hate having my picture taken and I loathe the sound of my voice when it is recorded. Add to this the fact that I am under the influence of much more than the fresh sea air blowing in off the Pacific and it should surprise no one that I begin acting like Louis Farrakhan at a press conference when somebody asks him why he abandoned his promising calypso career.

Sweating profusely (the makeup never stood a chance), and consulting with my Inner Attorney at length before carefully answering each question (some people cater to their "inner child"—which keeps their "inner pedophile" both busy and satisfied—I cater to my Inner Attorney), the result was one of the lamest conversations I've ever had. The Reporter, who has the only "off-camera" face I can identify with any certainty given her propinquity to me, away from the lights, feeds me precomposed questions having to do with my penis, penises in general, my and their functionality, legal drugs available by prescription, illegal drugs available at raves, and bizarre and unnatural combinations of all of the above. Despite the nerves and the booze, my responses are measured and conservative. I do, after all, have an application in with the San Francisco Police Department. Hell, someday I might want to run for public office. It simply won't do to confess to torrid and cardinal sins on television.

I don't remember exactly what questions were asked. In fact, I remember only two things about the entire interview:

1. After asking me a question, the Reporter begins nodding slowly and hyperdramatically, the way a parent would nod encouragingly to a child trying to read his or her first sentence. Having subsequently been subjected to other similar on-camera interviews with different reporters for different shows, I can tell you with some authority that all TV reporters do this, and its purpose is functionally identical to the parent/child reading nod: The Reporter is drawing out your response, rewarding each word with a nod of appreciation, thus encouraging a continuation of

the flow of words, which words will be rewarded by even deeper and more dramatic nods. At one point in the interview, when we are speaking of a completely hypothetical situation, my Inner Attorney allows me to speak freely, which I do. After holding forth for about 45 seconds (which is an eternity for television interviews), the Reporter's head is nodding so ridiculously and almost violently that it appears in this weird light as if she has lost interest in my response and has begun fellating some part of the camera.

2. After virtually every response I give, despite what I think are my successful attempts at walking the ultrafine line between brutal truth and drunken sincerity and good old self-preservation, and despite what I assume are his efforts at restraint, Kristoffer audibly fails to stifle snickers of varying intensity, which snickers, coming from the nebulous darkness of the "off-camera" world, thoroughly rattle me and piss me off and remind me that this whole thing is just ridiculous beyond description.

The interview seems to go on for hours, but in actuality takes less than 30 minutes. The wave of relief that washes over me when the Reporter folds up her question sheet and says, smiling, "That's all I've got," and the Camera Guy shuts off his killer klieg lights and his wife the Sound Girl withdraws her menacing stick and its pendulous black attachment from the airspace directly above my cranium is almost equal to the relief I felt when I woke a few nights earlier to the realization that the fear that I had penetrated Roseanne Barr was just another in a series of horrible dreams.

I have no idea to what sins I have confessed on tape, or what sort of hyperlibidinous drug demon I will be made out to be after this Lipshitz character gets done doing dark deeds in his editing bay. And I don't care. It's over. And now comes the Real Fun. It is time to strap on the wireless mics and hit the town so that ABC can get footage of me and Kristoffer stalking around San Francisco interacting with women in nightclubs.

While the Camera Guy removes all the dimmers he had installed only an hour ago, the Sound Girl fits both Kristoffer and me with hidden body microphones.

A Quick Note About Hidden Body Microphones: These body mic units are simply tiny microphones that are clipped to one's collar or somewhere in the vicinity of one's mouth (assuming that is the orifice from which sonic emissions are to be recorded—which turns out to be a dangerous assumption, indeed, given what Kris does with his body mic during one particularly prodigiously flatulent visit to the men's room later in the evening) and connected to a transmitter that clips onto one's belt. The microphones are not actually intended to be hidden (only the cops can do that legally), but simply unobtrusive.

Kristoffer and I climb into the Reporter's car, and the crew couple climbs into their SUV and follows us to Tommy's Mexican Restaurant on Geary and 23rd, the proprietor of which I know and have called in advance to tell him about the news crew from ABC and "reserved" a space at the perpetually packed tequila bar.

Indeed, Tommy's son Julio rousts two customers from their perches at the bar so that these two white boys with dreadlocks and a camera crew can sit and sip their expensive margaritas (rocks, no salt) that have already been prepared and are waiting for us. As great as the margaritas are, I'd rather stick to the schnapps, just to maintain a theme and avoid the inevitable antemeridian cephalgia that mixing one's booze brings, but what the hell.

This treatment makes me feel like a colossal asshole for having usurped these people's barstools, paying customers who, by all rights, were there first and had much more legitimacy with their asses on these stools than we did with ours. But, the presence of the camera crew affects the people at the bar strongly, and they become curious and almost deferential to us, even though they have no idea who we are or that we are completely undeserving of such treatment.

But, Kristoffer and I are also toweringly drunk and rapidly getting even more so as the pricey agave flows freely, the cost of which is going directly onto the Reporter's ABC Television corporate credit card. Soon the margarita-fueled curiosity gets the better of three nubile coeds who are so frighteningly stereotypical in their dyed-blond Californianess that it is laughable, and will thus not be detailed here.

"So, like, who *are* you guys?" the first one bubbles. Kristoffer shoots me a look that I have become all too familiar with through the years. He has the uncanny ability to glare at me in this certain way that clearly communicates all of the following simultaneously:

1. Whatever you're thinking, don't.
2. Please, I am *begging* you: think . . . I mean really *think* before you speak.
3. Remember what happened the last time you ignored the Glare.

4. You are an idiot with no moral barometer when you are sober, and things only go south when you are drunk, and you are reprehensibly drunk.

5. For fuck's sake have a heart. It's never too late to develop a conscience.

6. I don't know why I bother: I'd have better luck counseling Caligula.

7. Hopeless. You are utterly fucking hopeless, and you deserve everything you get. I am *not* bailing you out of jail this time.

8. Fucker.

I process all of this and take it to heart. He is correct on every point.

I open my mouth to tell this girl the truth about *20/20* and Viagra and so on, but at the last second, my Inner Attorney, who is six sheets to the wind and now wearing a toga, yells clearly and without reserve, "Fuck it!"

"We're in a band called, uh . . . Bitch Casket, and these guys are from MTV." Kristoffer, who was mid-sip, gags and chokes and spews booze through his nose. I kick him in the leg, and he grabs a napkin, covers his face, and heads for the head.

"All the publicity lately has really gotten to his nerves. The poor guy is just a wreck . . . all the publicity and money."

Sudden movement at the other end of the bar catches my attention: It is the Sound Girl and her headphones, who is laughing so hard that she appears to be having an epileptic fit. *Oh shit . . . the mics . . . this is all on tape!*

My Inner Attorney has laid his head down on my Inner Bar and simply raises his right arm with the middle finger extended and mumbles some incoherent gibberish that concludes with an exuberant: ". . . so let it flyyyyyyy!"

The girl's friends are now gathered around and they all seem sincerely interested. The Sound Girl is looking at me as if to say, "It's your grave . . . dig away."

"So yeah, we're Bitch Casket, and our first album is about to be released here in the states, and MTV is doing a documentary on us. The record's already in the Top 10 in Europe."

The first girl has cocked her head to the side, arched her back, and is spinning a strand of hair with her left index finger, blatantly displaying the lack of any sort of ring that would indicate attachment. "Bitch Casket, huh? I think I've heard of you guys . . . it sounds familiar. What's the name of your record?"

I glance furtively at the Sound Girl, whose eyes are shut tightly, bracing herself against what's coming.

"It's called *Beating a Dead Whore*."

The Sound Girl collapses onto the floor somewhere behind the bar, out of sight.

"Do they play your stuff on the radio yet here? Like, will we hear your songs?"

"Yeah . . . oh yeah . . . the record company is having trouble picking the single . . . they like them all. I think they have it narrowed down to three: 'Up Against the Wall Motherfucker,' 'Acres of Penis,' and . . . oh, what's the other one they like? Oh yeah: 'Have Some Marijuana.' That one's really popular in Amsterdam."

I'm about to see if this mini-harem would like to join us for an evening of clubbing when Kristoffer returns from the bathroom, red-faced, with a grimace the psychogenesis of which is either from the steaming heap of lies he knows I've been laying on this poor gullible girl and her cohorts, or from what must have been the agonizing pain of blowing *añejo* through his nasal cavity, or most likely, a twisted combination of both.

Fortunately for all parties concerned, the bar is very small and very limiting for the Camera Guy with regard to angles and lighting and such, and it is decided that we are going to leave. The girl gives me her digits as we depart and does that cute little "call me" signal by wiggling her thumb and her pinkie near her mouth and ear. I'm strangely charmed.

Our next stop is a goth club on Folsom Street, which club I commonly refer to as "The Night of the Living Ex-Girlfriends." which moniker pretty much explains my entire motivation for wanting to show up there with the news crew and ABC's expense account. Just a little "fuck you" to a few girls who had sought greener (or in their über-dramatic goth cases, *blacker*) pastures, which pastures I can pretty much guarantee did not have national news crews tailing them. But this venue is quickly nixed by the Camera Guy, who claims that there is so little light in the club that they would probably get more interesting footage if he simply left the lens cap on. I take umbrage at this for no good reason, but the Reporter buys me a shot of schnapps, and the revolution is quelled.

This particular part of Folsom Street is called "The Corridor" and is known for its numerous nightclubs and concert venues, so there are half-a-dozen other places within a block or two to choose from. The Camera Guy investigates two or three venues before finding the "best bet" for lighting and camera angles and so forth, and that's fine. I trust his judgment. He is a professional. However, the one he chooses is an ultra-trendy quasi-rave club peopled mostly by twenty-somethings working in entry-level positions in the advertising industry, all of them bonded together by their shared contempt for the work they do and for the people they work for, all of them just as equally bonded together by their collective delusion that they are each using this same loathsome industry as an almost requisite stepping stone toward their just-as-collective goal to each ultimately direct feature films and be forced to hire bodyguards to keep them from being hit in the head by the heavy and prestigious awards, which will be so plentiful that it will seem like Hollywood is raining trophies and accolades upon them.

I used to be one of these people.

I also used to shit my pants and throw applesauce and communicate by crying. But at some point, we all must see the Light, or smell the Stench, or both, and grow up and become forever realistic and jaded (these terms are synonyms in the ad industry).

And, I don't want to be seen on national television schmoozing with any of these thinly veiled yuppies anymore than I want to be seen crapping my pants or throwing applesauce or any of the rest of it. But, it is not my call, and I can see they do have a well-stocked bar and the ABC corporate card is still presumably valid, so why not? In we go.

Nearly enemies not an hour ago, Kristoffer and I are now suddenly united in our hatred of this place. After all, it was in the miasma of the advertising world that we first met, and it was only with the encouragement and support of each other that we were able to escape that soul-sucking black hole of art and culture.

Grumpily, we get our schnapps and maneuver to a corner to talk shit and sneer at those around us. I'm not sure if it's the additional libations or his unabashed odium of these people and what they represent, but suddenly Kris is in total support of using the presence of the film crew and its focus on us as leverage for separation, and an indication of apartness and implied superiority.

Regrettably, the effect is not as strong and deference-inspiring as it had been with those bimbettes back at Tommy's. These people work in television, albeit making commercials in which frogs sell beer, but they know that the mere presence of a film crew in-and-of-itself doesn't mean dick. Our plight is seeming desperate and we are discussing the implementation of a "scorched-bar" policy to retaliate for being dragged, cruelly and against our wills, into the horrible yuppie powwow, by not talking to anyone except the bartender, from whom we shall order a round of schnapps for the whole bar and a few for ourselves, and drink them in as short a time as possible in the hope of getting a second round going before the Camera Guy et al. figure out what's going on. We have, of course, again forgotten about the goddamn body mics and their privacy-raping presence, and are being viciously reminded of this by a laserlike glare from the Sound Girl when something just this side of miraculous occurs.

An especially attractive assistant producer for one of the largest ad agencies in the city, with whom both Kris and I have worked, and after whom pretty much every heterosexual male in the business has lusted and watched the ass of whenever she leaves, comes bouncing up, *avec* an equally cute and equally female friend, and begins just shooting the shit with us like we're roommates who happened to bump into each other during respective nights on the town. Neither one of us has seen

this girl in at least a year and even then she was coolly cordial
at best—completely uninterested on any level in either one of
us. But we are guys and we have been sucking down schnapps
and cocktails for, hell, about three hours now, and we really
don't give much of a damn about the past and don't mind their
company at all. The Camera Guy moves quickly and strategi-
cally and gets his shots. Because we do sort-of know her, and
because she is probably a very decent person, and because we
do still share some friends, I don't even start in with the MTV
Bitch Casket bullshit and I give her the real deal about *20/20*
and Viagra and Ecstasy, and she begins to think that perhaps
she doesn't want to appear across the screens of America in this
context, and makes a quick, typically "cordial" exit off camera.
*Gutless ho . . . I don't want to appear on television like this either,
but here I am. It's for the Cause. Obviously, that was something she
would never be able to comprehend.*

And with that, the Reporter and crew call it a night. Kris
and I hurriedly chug our fresh row of drinks and stumble out to
the crew's SUV, where the Sound Girl removes the body mics.

The Reporter gives us a ride home, of which ride I have no
recollection. I was beyond drunk. I was *faced*. Kristoffer, weigh-
ing less than I do, but having matched my intake drink for
drink that evening, is in a drooling stupor in the backseat, making his presence known every minute or two with Wagnerianly
loud, multioctave belches that cause the car to smell like the
beer garden at the state fair in the morning after the final night's
blowout. The Reporter takes it all in stride—she actually seems
happy. I don't know if it's because this sinister night is coming
to a close, or because she actually had more fun on this story
than she would have had covering some latch-hook convention

in Tulare or something. Maybe she's just relieved that I never
tried to dry-hump her leg.

Pulling up to my apartment building, we thank each other
and wish each other well in future endeavors as I pull the gas-
trointestinally explosive Kristoffer from the backseat where he
has slumped down and continues to drool. The cold San Francisco night air revives him a bit and gives him what must be
about his 23rd wind as he belches his general well-wishing at
the Reporter who smiles and waves and drives off back to Marin.

That should have been that, and if there was any sort of
benevolent power that gives a damn about the state of the universe, the night would have ended there. But you know it did
not.

The superintendent of the building next door to mine evidently changed all the fluorescent bulbs in his building and set
the used ones out on the sidewalk to be picked up. I don't think
he or anyone else intended for it to be Kristoffer who picked
them up, but that's what he just did. I don't even bother to ask
what nefarious and pernicious devices are brewing in that
crude, schnapps-soaked psyche of his: The eyes are focused and
dangerous, and it is clear he is not to be interfered with.

He zips up the stairs with startling agility for someone whose
liver has been marinating in toxins for hours. By the time I climb
the three flights of stairs to my place, I can hear that Kris already
has scaled the next two flights, which take one to the door that
opens onto the roof. When I hear the roof door slam shut, I am
torn. Do I go inside my apartment, lock all five locks behind me,
eat a handful of Somas, and let Kristoffer go with God? Or, do I
simply resign myself to my lot in life, and trudge up two more
flights to bear witness to whatever chaos is about to happen?

I put my key into my dead bolt and decide that whatever havoc Kristoffer is going to inflict does not need any help from me, when I hear the explosion. I pull my key out of the lock like a john whose condom has just broken and scurry begrudgingly up two more flights to the roof.

Kristoffer assumes an overtly manly pose and he is holding one of the four-foot fluorescent bulbs in his right hand like a javelin, poised to throw.

"What the fuck are you doing, Kristoffer?"

"I am not Kristoffer," he yells. "I am *Zeus!* I have thrown a lightning bolt down at that pitiful planet of puny mortals below, and I am preparing to throw another one."

Christ, I thought. The SWAT team has already probably been dispatched. Something needs to be done before the news crews start showing up. I'll have to talk him down. Gently. Rationally. Calmly.

"You stupid fucking schnapps-sucking Nazi! You *are* Kristoffer and you *are* mortal, and you *are* about to become a multiple felon and some *real* criminal's bitch. Now get away from the edge of my roof before your drunk ass falls off. Besides, it's starting to rain."

"BLASPHEMER!" he yells, this time loud enough to produce an urban echo. "I *know* it's raining! I am making it rain. I am *Zeus,* and I am pissing on you and all other mortals. The earth is my urinal, and I piss on the weak and infirm!"

Without dropping the fluorescent bulb, he manages to undo his belt, button, and fly, and does, in fact, launch his golden arc of transcendence.

For the first time in our friendship, it is I who is giving him the Glare. And he is impervious.

"Urinal cake mortals! You are unworthy to suck the balls of the gods. Prepare to feel the wrath of Zeus!"

His pants fall down heavily around his ankles as he hoists the bulb back to throw.

From the darkness below, from the void over the edge that I cannot see from where I am standing, I hear a window slam open, and a hauntingly familiar voice begins cursing at him in Russian.

Kristoffer's golden current is still flowing strongly as he chucks his fluorescent tube downward into the darkness, not actually *at* her, but close enough to make me smile, and the result is dramatic: an appropriately thunderous explosion and the sound of breaking glass pierces the otherwise quiet San Francisco night. No more screaming Russian. And now he is holding *two* bulbs—a two-fisted god. And the rain really begins to come down. Hell, maybe he *is* Zeus. Who am I to judge? He's the one with the lightning bolts. And if he's hurling them at the brown-toenailed Slav below, he can call himself whatever he wants as far as I'm concerned. Just because a man is standing on a rooftop in the rain with his drawers around his ankles does not preclude divinity. Nor does the sound of approaching sirens. But that is enough for me to make an escape; this is no longer my problem. Let Frisco's Finest deal with the pants-less Greek deity on the roof. It is Soma time, and I am going to bed.

The next morning, another one of Ted Lipshitz's damned Eastern Standard Time phone calls jangles me awake.

"Mmmmhello?"

"Jayson—Ted Lipshitz. How'd it go?"

I'm still asleep. Hell, I'm still drunk. *How'd what go?* And then it all comes rushing back like the pavement toward the face of a hapless skateboarder with inner-ear problems: the booze, the weed, the phallocentric interview, the body mics, the drunken claims of rock stardom and MTV documentation, the cold-shouldered yuppies, Zeus.

I look around the apartment. No sign of Kristoffer, Zeus, or any personality other than mine.

"Fine. Things went fine. It was fun."

"Terrific. Glad to hear it."

"Ted, listen . . . you're not going to make me out to be too much of an idiot, are you?"

He chuckles: "I won't make you look bad. I know you'll blast us in some magazine if we do."

I chuckle politely but curtly, to let him know that he is correct. The pen is mightier than the videotape, and I've got a lot of pens on my desk. They are next to my day planner, on which today's To Do list is scrawled a reminder to remember my middle name, which I do. I take a mighty pen and check the "Completed" box next to it.

20/20 airs the night before Valentine's Day. It is scheduled for 9:00 p.m. in San Francisco. I am running dangerously low on tranquilizers of any vintage, and so I must save what I have for what will surely be the post-show stress storm. I am going to have to endure the viewing sober.

The phone calls start around 6:00 p.m. when it is 9:00 p.m. on the East Coast and begin with the Boston branch of the Gallaway family, where some aunt or uncle or cousin had happened to be channel surfing and happened to see me and called every single other aunt, uncle, or cousin into the room, or on the phone, and said something like, "Quick! Turn on Channel 7 . . . Jayson's on *20/20* talking about drugs and his penis!" Once the story finished, I am told there were several family rooms in the greater Boston area with my relatives crowded around their TVs, wide-eyed and gape-mouthed, and no one saying a word. That's when someone decided to pick up the phone. One particular uncle whose love of tipple is the stuff of familial legend has elected himself spokesman.

"Hello?"

"Are you out of your fucking mind?"

I haven't talked to this guy in like, three years. I feign ignorance.

"You! On the TV! On *my* TV! Talking about your *penis!* You take Viagra?"

Christ.

"No, I don't take Viagra. I *took* Viagra once and I wrote some goofy story about it, and it got published and now everybody thinks I'm some kind of expert."

"So you're not an expert?"

"Hell no. I'm just an idiot with a word processor."

"Then quit talking about your dick and get off the television!"

It goes on like this for half an hour, a new call coming every five minutes or so. And just when it starts dying down and there is a lull on the phone, Round Two begins at 7:00 p.m., when the heinous thing airs on Central Time. Another telephonic chain of harangues begins. I defend myself as best I can, but I haven't even seen the goddamn thing yet.

One of the calls that comes during the eight o'clock hour is from my mother. I assume my drunken uncle has called to berate her for conceiving me, but no . . . a military cargo plane has crashed in Sacramento where my parents live, and the local ABC affiliate has interrupted regularly scheduled programming to report live from the scene. Salvation does indeed have many unusual faces, and in this case, its face is a huge fireball from which no one is believed to have survived. Terrible for the crew and their families, terrific for me and mine. Even though I'll be taping the show, I've learned my lesson from the previous two hours and I unplug my phone.

Everything is nearly jeopardized when the ABC station in San Francisco mentions a "breaking story" about a downed military aircraft in Sacramento during an interstitial newsbreak, concluding with the newscaster threatening to break in to scheduled programming as events warrant.

Oh *hell* no. *God, if you just crashed a huge plane into my hometown just to pre-empt my national television debut, my televised 15 minutes of shame, You'd better watch Your ass. My best friend is Zeus, and if You preempt Our show, You're going to have both of us on Your ass. And he's got fluorescent lights.*

If He did hear my prayer, He apparently didn't like it very much. The ABC affiliate in San Francisco interrupts programming at 8:55 p.m., five minutes before *20/20,* to go "live now to our network affiliate in Sacramento, to the scene of a cargo-plane disaster for the latest details . . ."

Disaster? *Great.*

Sumbitch.

There I stood, in front of my television, using both hands to point my remote at the VCR, fingers on the triggers of REC and PLAY, waiting, like a SWAT team sniper, for something to happen.

A C-5 cargo plane taking off from Mather Air Force Base crashed into a nearby junkyard, and burst into a fireball, instantly killing the half-dozen-or-so crew members.

Terrible.

But that's the whole story. Fewer than ten people dead, an old airplane destroyed (and crashing in about as perfect a place as possible in terms of cleanup: a junkyard), and now nothing but pictures of wrecked airplane and burning garbage. The end. So let's get back to regularly scheduled programming, please.

But no. The affiliate's reporter is just droning on (as they always do) about what they *don't* know (the names of the airmen killed, the cause of the crash, and so on) and how they won't know these things for at least a day or two.

I look at the crucifix my mother recently gave me in a last-ditch attempt to save my ever-darkening soul from eternal ruination. To placate her, and to roll the dice with the everlasting salvation bit, I had hung the thing in a place of honor, just over the TV, centered (after many failed attempts and cussing) perfectly on the wall. Jesus was well hung. But still I'm looking at smoldering debris. And there's Jesus, just looking down lifelessly at the TV beneath him.

Never mind the ass-kissy prayers of the Catholic Church . . . I'm siding with the Old Testament Jews who weren't afraid to chew God's ass if things weren't going well. The divine abhors obsequiousness. Sometimes you need to punctuate your prayers with a bit of menace. And this is, evidently, one of those times.

"Well, don't just *hang* there, hippie . . . *do something!* Miracle some sense into the programming director's head. Just do something. *Anything!*"

The reporter sums up what she doesn't know; the local station kills the live feed; and the local anchor returns to regularly scheduled programming, which programming is a douche commercial. I wink at Jesus.

The douche commercial ends, and *20/20* begins.

I quickly find out why Jesus was so interested in making sure tonight's show airs, and it has nothing to do with me. Jesus is being featured on this evening's show, just after me. Yep. Some guy who is claiming to be Jesus, who really does look like our Lord and Savior (kind eyes, long brown hair, beard, robe fastened with a rope belt, sandals, the whole bit). I can't tell from the brief preshow overview if he has functioning stigmata or not—I suppose it would be rude to ask. But yes, Jesus is back and living somewhere in the Pacific Northwest.

Two thoughts occur to me simultaneously:

1. If ABC is going to give this granola-eating peacenik an interview, the Reporter and crew should have stuck around for Kris's rooftop transformation into Zeus. It would be much more interesting. Kris actually dropped his pants . . . I doubt Jesus is going to rip open his robe and reveal his holy scepter to the prime-time audience.

2. If my mom, fervent Irish Catholic that she is, gets really pissed off about this whole thing and wants me out of the will, I can always point to the fact that I was on the same show as Jesus . . . in fact I was on *before* Jesus. That should make her feel a little better.

Abruptly the footage of Jesus ends and there is a shot of a Viagra pill, and I brace for impact. *Wham!* There I am, sucking back schnapps and chatting up yuppie chicks about the Ivory Shaft.

Ugh.

I start pacing and sweating. I smile. I grit my teeth in a rictus and make my eyes bulge. I don't know how to feel. Is this going to be some sort of professional coup? Will my phone be ringing off the hook for the rest of forever with offers of lucrative development deals, or offers to star in television pilots and reality television shows? Or, will this be the end of life as I know it: the death of Cool? Will there be protesters outside my building, armed with fruit for throwing?

There are other stories before mine, and this angers me greatly. I want to get this over with. Let the hammer fall.

Soon enough, it does.

The anchor doing the story appears and begins talking about Valentine's Day and seasonal romance, and quickly segues into Viagra. The video switches to a commercial from a few years back when Bob Dole was pimping the little blue diamonds. There is Bob in all his horror: old, wrinkled, and saggy, telling everybody that Little Bob was just as old, wrinkled, and saggy, until he started eating these magical fruits of Pfizer. And then, in an intentionally brutal and jarring contrast, appears yrs. truly. There I am, unwrinkled, about 50 years younger than Bob, the sides of my head shaved, dreadlocks on top tied in back like some weird Rastafarian Mohawk, wearing a black see-through shirt. Contrasted to Mr. Dole, it was obvious I had been living in San Francisco for too long.

As my weirdness filled the screen, the anchor spoke the words to the nation that would haunt me for the rest of my exponentially increasingly pathetic life: "Meet the *new* face of Viagra: Jayson Gallaway."

Mother of God! With that one sentence, I had replaced Bob

Dole as the spokesmodel for Viagra. I had just become the poster child for erectile dysfunction.

I wanted to pick up the phone and yell. I wanted to know how much Bob Dole had been paid for his commercial. How much could it have been? $100,000? Half a mill? It sure as shit was more than a couple bottles of schnapps!

I happened to glance at the crucifix, and I swear I saw Jesus grinning wryly, hanging still.

God could not help me now. Schnapps could not help me now. My only hope was my stash of Valium. All of it.

I woke up around noon the next day, rested, peaceful. The sun was shining pleasantly. It took a moment for the memory of the previous night's debacle to return. In the amnesiac haze induced by excessive Valium, I had at some point bonded the crucifix to my TV screen—upside down—and apparently tried to throw the whole works out of my apartment window, Keith Richards style. Fortunately for all parties concerned, I had been too drugged out to carry the TV more than a foot or two, and had done a piss-poor job of gluing, and all damage was quickly undone.

There were 37 messages on my voice mail. I deleted them all without listening.

Eventually, later that afternoon, I dared to venture outside. There were no picketers wielding produce. No one screamed anything at me from passing cars.

As I walked down the street, a cute girl with a bag of groceries walked by and smiled.

Things seemed like they might be okay.

The Whore of the Ring

Just like any other drug that elevates any aspect or level of performance, Viagra has a pretty harsh comedown, so to speak. After having an erection as solid as a petrified oak for 12 hours straight, your regular ol' boner just ain't the same. Think Nerf Bat compared to croquet mallet. At worst, it's disappointing, and disappointment of any kind is simply not something for which my penis or my psyche were ever wired. And yet, there is the brutal truth of the sober boner: no more sempiternal stiffies. No more genitalia that could also be used for home defense. Just an average, slightly gravity-defying flesh tube that at some moments is as soft as a sponge, and at other, better times, has the solidity of thawed pepperoni. It's okay, I guess. But who the hell wants thawed pepperoni when they could have frozen kielbasa? And since becoming the "new face of Viagra," I've had a bit of a reputation to live up to. (My parents are unspeakably proud. In fact, they no longer speak to me at all.)

So I called my doctor.

My doctor is a special man with a preternatural sense of impending doom with regard to me (as indicated in litigation-avoiding detail in my medical file) and an appreciation and understanding of the difference between the way things are supposed to be and the Way Things Are. He knows of my dark and squalid history, my aggressive disposition, and my complete lack of common sense and good judgment. He also knows I live in a world very different from his, which he once described as "a place where the devil plays show tunes on an accordion while angels floss their teeth." I have no idea what that means, and neither did he the next morning when the acid finally wore off. But the gist is that he knows I have friends in places so dark their eyesight has become modified, and that I have access to virtually any chemical or pseudopharmaceutical of any significance in modern Western medicine. And it is because of all this that he knows when I do actually call him for something, it is an act of desperation. He is the Last Resort.

Most of the doctor's incoming calls are taken as messages by the front-office help, to be returned during his "phone hours" of 6:00 and 7:00 p.m. My calls are put right through.

"Jayson . . . how ya doing?" He has an urgency about him whenever he talks to me that I imagine he doesn't have when he communicates with anyone else. It is the tone of a hostage negotiator who has had too much coffee. I suspect when his secretary tells him that I am on the phone, he runs to his plush office and begins flipping cable news channels, looking for breaking stories or checking to see if there is a camera trained on me hanging from the Golden Gate Bridge, wearing nothing but a smile and a belt of Semtex with a boom box set up nearby blaring Gary Glitter's "Rock and Roll Part 2," and demanding chocolate doughnuts Or Else.

"I was taking Viagra and now I'm not, and I'm disappointed in the results."

"Why the hell did you take Viagra? I didn't write you a scrip for Viagra."

"An experiment . . . research . . . work. I got it off the Internet."

"Gosh darn all this new technology. Nothing but trouble. It's going to be the downfall of this entire nation, you mark my words. If you were having erectile problems, you could have come to me. I thought we had a relationship here. What else have you gotten from the Internet? Jesus! What can you get? Heroin? Crack? Are there no limits? Are you on crack?"

"Would you calm down, please? No, I'm not on crack. And I *wasn't* having erectile problems! Like I said, it was an experiment. Never mind. What do I do?"

"Are you saying you can't get an erection?"

"Say that again and I'll break your jaw. I know where you sleep."

"Well, what *exactly* is the problem?

"It's just not the same."

"Well, of course it's not the same, dipshit, it's like . . ."

"Dipshit? Did they teach you that in medical school? Did you go to medical school?"

"It's like when you take Ecstasy, and then you don't. You feel different than you did. That's the whole point of taking drugs."

"So what are you telling me? That I have to keep taking boner pills?"

"I should tell you yes. I should say, 'Yes, Jayson, if you ever want to have anything remotely resembling an erection that won't be mocked and taunted by anyone you might trick into being in the room with you while naked, yes, you must take boner pills every day with breakfast for the rest of your otherwise limp life.' And I should also refuse to write you a scrip for that or anything else. Let you go surf your precious little Internet. See how far that gets you."

"You are a dick, and you have the ethics of a goat."

"Hey, I'm not the one on the phone with wang problems."

"Ass."

"So do you want a prescription or what?"

"No. Well . . . I mean if I can get some Oxys . . ."

"I swear to Christ if you're on a cordless phone I'm hanging up. People can hear these conversations on cordless phones, you know. Baby monitors pick them up."

"Just a joke, doc. Shit. When did you get so uptight? No, I don't want any goddamn Viagra. I want to know if there is any treatment for Post-Viagra Stress Disorder?"

"PVSD—nice. I'm going to use that. Publish a study. Get rich."

"Stay on topic please."

"Well . . . hmmm. Do you know what a cock ring is?"

"I am *not* piercing my unit. Nor will I pierce anything in the vicinity. There is a 'No-Fly' zone in the zone of my fly which is strictly off-limits to anything sharp or pointy."

"Good Lord, Jayson, where did you grow up?"

"What's that got to do with anything?"

"You are just so suburban sometimes. Look, a cock ring is just that: a ring that goes around your cock, and it constricts the flow of blood. Blood flows in, your penis becomes engorged, the ring becomes tight, and it keeps the blood from flowing back out. Simple. Any adult bookstore will have a selection of them."

"Is this a gay thing?"

"Do you want it to be? Will you be having sex with a man?"

"Did I mention I know where you sleep?"

"Are you propositioning me?"

"I hate you. Kiss my ass."

"Doctor/patient relationships are ethically frowned upon. Besides, I'm straight. I have no interest in kissing your ass or any other part of you."

"I'm getting another doctor."

"I know several gay doctors who would take you as a patient."

"I truly do hate you. I hope you get a parasite."

"Oh lighten up. You need to learn to laugh more. Just get a cock ring. Let me know how it works."

That evening, just after sunset, I am walking down Geary Blvd. toward Frenchy's, one of the most heavily trafficked and accessible-without-certainty-of-being-mugged adult bookstores in San Francisco, a city known as much for its contributions to the sex industry as it is for fog and cable cars.

Any embarrassment or shame or urge to don a black trench coat, hat, and sunglasses when patronizing such establishments went out the window with me long ago when I realized that any acquaintance whom I might run into between the rows of dildos and rubberized fists and pregnant gangbang videos would, patently, have to be guiltily there as well. And besides, at this point any reports to family members of Jayson sightings in such nefarious places would be received with, at best, a sarcastic "No shit"—at worst, an eye roll expressing utter inner despair and hopelessness with regard to my moral and social standing.

Whatever glassblower got the contract for this place must have simply ablated his annual profit projections on this store alone. Frenchy's uses neon the way the Vatican uses marble. The red-and-blue glow emitted by the various signs ("Private Preview Booths—25 Cents," "Open 24/7/365," etc.) can be seen in the satellite photos on nightly Bay Area television weather reports. One can actually read by this light up to a block away (this is true . . . I've actually done it, examining a receipt during a speed-fueled paranoia spell in which I was convinced that I had been charged double for my copy of *Lactating Latinas Volume 6*).

There are always two or three black men loitering immediately outside the building. I say "black" rather than "African-American" because I suspect that if my lily-white ass were to stand out here long enough, I too would be black after about a week. You can *tan* off of this neon. Really. The "black" people never ask for money; in fact, they never say anything at all. They just stand there, leaning against the entryway at various angles, eyeing passersby with eyes that are Golem-like in their whiteness. One suspects these are transplanted retirees from Florida who are jonesing for the Sarasota sunshine and have discovered a way to circumvent the costliness of California's tanning beds.

Previously relaxed irises are slammed tightly upon entering the perpetually garishly fluorescently lit "bookstore." Curious name, really: There is not a single book to be found anywhere in here. Not one. Magazines, dear God yes, there are glossy magazines of every abominable vintage, catering to every imaginable fetish. There are all the standards, of course: *Hustler, Penthouse, Swank,* and so on. There are magazines dedicated to the themes of unnaturally busty women, almost unnaturally small-breasted women, women over 40, over 50, over 60 (which, by the way, !),

forklift-strainingly obese women ("Pick a roll, any roll!"),
anorexic crack addicts whose sexuality seems almost incidental,
pregnant women, black women, Very Black Women, women
with comically disproportionately large butts, a whole section of
magazines featuring nothing but women's feet—some clean and
carefully manicured and polished posed against pristine white
backgrounds, some standing in piles of cow shit in the middle of
European pastures. Brunettes with brown eyes. Women smoking cigarettes. Women with poochie bellies that hang slightly
over tight jeans from beneath equally tight half-shirts. Girls with
pigtails. Girls wearing glasses and business attire. Here's a copy
of *Just 18* that features some of my finest prose (see "The Art of
Darkness," p. 186).

Assuming all of the aforementioned smut is directed at an
essentially heterosexual demographic, to the right is an equally
sizable and diverse homosexual magazine section. There are two
basic reasons why I don't spend much time studying this section: First, I am incorrigibly heterosexual; second, what I see on
the covers of the top row is both disturbing and humbling . . .
complex-inducingly humbling. I've never had any complaints
with regard to adequacy or size in my sexual experiences, but
god*damn!* Some of these Brobdingnagian brothers are practically
deformed. They must have trouble just *getting around.* Unless the
pictures are substantially Photoshopped (which I suspect and
hope and pray is the case for purely personal reasons), basic
locomotion would be at least impeded, if not damn near impossible. In the name of ethics and solid journalism, and perhaps a
bit of self-esteem preservation, I linger long enough to find some
semblance of balance in the gay section. It doesn't take long:
guys with freakishly small penises. Guys with freakishly small

penises who enjoy being tied up, slathered in lube, and put on the receiving end of physical liaisons with numerous other men at the same time (*The Knotty Boys—Tie Them Up, Tie Them Down—More Holes Than a Golf Course, The Knotty Boys—All Male Ex-Con Bitch Slap Gang Bang*).

Indeed.

Enough of the magazines. There are movies to which I must attend.

Whenever in the video section of a porn store, I am reminded of a day in college when the guest speaker for my human-sexuality class was an FBI agent. He was the sort of law-enforcement agent that you suspect *might* have existed in the United States in the '50s, but certainly not now. Yet there he was, speaking with grave severity and not a pinch of irony about the direct connection between the viewing of pornography and deviant criminal behavior. Ted Bundy had planted the blame for his crimes against humanity squarely on the hunched and trench-coated shoulders of pornography, and this guy from the FBI could not have agreed more. He described with utter disgust, and lips trembling with barely contained rage, the way videotaped perversions are actually *categorized* (Can you believe it?) by subject (or "fetish" as he put it), and proceeded to list a few of these categories in the same manner that an overdramatic prosecuting attorney from Alabama would list the defendant's crimes in a made-for-TV movie about a black man accused of raping a white woman: in short, he *seethed*. When I questioned his conclusion that the simple viewing of X-rated material leads unquestionably to deviant criminal behavior with particular regard to the fact that he had obviously spent many an hour viewing this material (in the name of justice and professional mastery, of course), just how he had found the strength to come crawling out of the gutter of filth that is adult entertainment with his federal badge still gleaming, he adeptly skirted the question and suggested an after-class chat, which chat I suspect was to get my name and social-security number with the sole purpose of putting my wise ass on a federal watch list of potential sex criminals. So I let it slide and made an escape just before class was over.

Call me a criminal deviant if you'd like, but I appreciate the categorization. It is no different from any "normal" video store. They have categories. How the hell else is one supposed to navigate the ever-growing sea of videotaped entertainment? Mr. FBI found it fiendish and abhorrent. I find it convenient. So much for me, I suppose, but I, like everyone else, have likes and dislikes in all areas, whether it is vegetables, luxury automobiles, or filth films. But these *are* some pretty exotically named genres, no matter how you look at it: All-Girl, Anal, Gonzo, Gang Bang, Asian, Bondage, Amateur, Fisting, Anal-to-Oral, Golden Showers, Scat, Vomit, and so on. There is a section called *Bukkake* that space, time, common decency, and editorial insistence prevent me from describing at all. But *Good Lord!,* if you've ever wanted real evidence, as in actual videotaped *proof* that humans, despite their inspired achievements, have, at least on certain levels, not only not evolved at all from the lower primates but actually taken a few steps in the other direction, take a look at a Bukkake movie. I can't even define it here without having to put a parental warning sticker on the cover (which they may do anyway, but there is still hope), so you'll have to do your own research. If you are too embarrassed to go to an adult bookstore, ask someone at your next family get-together. Bring it up at Bible study.

It just occurred to me that I did not come in here to stare in curious and awestruck amazement and horror at Bukkake boxes. I came in here to buy a cock ring, goddamnit.

Okay, so where are they? Magazines, movies, stripper gear, and cheap lingerie, dildos ranging in size from the seemingly useless to the truly daunting. Esoteric electronic devices with clamps and screws and other unidentifiable parts that look like the socially acceptable byproducts of heinous experiments done on prisoners in Nazi Germany or Iraq. This is not what I'm looking for. Let's see . . . condoms, lubricants, "Love Kits" designed for couples, "naughty" games for bachelor and bachelorette parties ("Pin the Macho on the Man"), anatomically correct and sexually functional inflatable women, men, pigs, and sheep (I shit you not: it's called the "Love Ewe"). I really don't want to ask the heavily pierced and tattooed early-twenties girl behind the counter where I might find the cock rings, please, but it appears that's exactly what I'm going to have to do.

There is a strange, innate code of silence in adult bookstores. The approximately 98 percent of such an establishment's customer base, who are males of one sexual persuasion or another, all know the Code: Don't Say Shit. Say nothing to no one. Especially other customers. Of course, at least once a day some goddamn hetero couple will come in, usually drunk (your typical hetero woman will not even consider stepping into such sticky-floored showrooms unless plied with drink), and overcompensate for their fear and awkwardness by not just breaking the Silence, but by being really loud and thus blowing the Code all to hell and typically causing an exodus of all but the most hard-core perverts. But other than that, one must respect the Code. If you absolutely must speak, it had best be only to the person behind the Counter. The Counter is the Counter rather than simply "the counter" because it is always elevated two or three feet above floor level, making the customer feel like some eight-year-old idiot ordering an ice-cream cone, having to stand on his tiptoes and speak louder than he would like to overcome the height disparity. The problem with respect to people in my present situation is that you're not an eight-year-old idiot ordering ice cream. You are an over-18-year-old idiot getting a handful of tokens for the Happy Booths in the back room, or, in my case, getting ready to ask where I might find a cock ring. I am second in line for the Counter when I see them.

You must be fucking kidding me!

In this store full of overpriced vice, in this sordid den of retail iniquity with its swarthy, sweaty-palmed customers and disturbingly sticky floors, the one thing (other than tokens and the actual cassettes or discs one rents that correspond to the display boxes on the sales floor) that is kept behind the Counter is—you guessed it—cock rings.

Fortunately, the freak in front of me is purchasing a "realistic" (according to the colorfully designed box), battery-operated (which batteries, by the way, as also stated proudly by the box, are included), motorized vagina with (again, via the pompous box) remote control.

If I may digress for just a moment, at this point in today's events I was faced with a question that I still, right now, to this day, have been unable to answer. Remote controls usually are assigned to large, typically nonportable appliances (TVs, VCRs, etc.) that sit in one place while the user sits or walks or does whatever in a spatially substantially different place, making the journey to the appliance to modify its behavior (change the channel, press PLAY, whatever) inconvenient. It has been the subject of innumerable comedy routines that people will, when faced with a missing remote, go into a frenzied and lengthy search-and-rescue operation that inevitably takes exponentially more time and energy than simply getting up and changing the channel or pressing PLAY would have ever done. And, it is with that in mind that I wonder: What reason under God could there be for having a remote control for your mechanized vagina? I mean, I don't think it's an unfair assumption that if one is using a motorized vagina, even if one is absurdly endowed, one is pretty much at least within arm's length of the thing. And, given that your average mechanical vagina (average being represented by the one the guy in front of me longs to purchase) is about the size of a softball, successful use of it would require one to hold it, somehow. So, if you've got the thing in your hand and it is actually touching you, being literally as close to you as possible, what imaginable benefit could be derived from a remote control? Of course, now I am wondering just what aspect of the functionality the remote controls . . . wetness, calescence, vibration? The mind reels at the possibilities, and for a second I'm tempted to forfeit my place in line to go over and check one of these things out for myself. But no. The fact that I am shopping for cock rings is bad enough. At least there is some shabby nobility in the potential that my product is designed for use with another, real, unmechanized partner, one with natural warmth and a pulse and everything. So, in line I stay.

The store's policy regarding the purchase of such "intimate" items ("intimate" being defined here as any item into which you stick your dick), which policy is clearly intended to prevent potentially gruesome attempts to return merchandise, is evidently to pull the intimate item out of its box or original packaging right there on the Counter in front of God and everybody, insert the included batteries, and switch the damn thing on, verifying with witnesses that at the moment of purchase, this motorized vagina did, in fact, work, and that there is no earthly reason for this particular mechanical vagina to ever, *ever* be brought back into this store. Don't even try. You have a better chance of returning a mail-order bride to the government of Vietnam than you do this vagina.

I must say, and I think my fellow line standers, who all are watching this testing process with shared interest, would concur that for what is essentially a cosmetically glorified foam-rubber mushroom-shaped tube designed to be simply a receptacle for the fruits of purely onanistic pursuits, the business end of the thing *does* actually look, from both an anatomical and aesthetic perspective, pretty damn realistic. The "hair" aspect of the device I find deeply disturbing, however. I know that wig shops and hair-extension parlors boast about using real human hair. But the box (and by "box" I am referring here to the colorful cardboard and plastic container the vagina came in—by "came in" I mean . . . oh, to hell with it), which has, up until this point, not been the least bit shy about promoting every imaginably promotable feature of the thing in terms of realism remains silent on the issue. And that's fine with me. Given the number of these particular products on this sales floor, and assuming the same number are available in other stores, and knowing the approximate number of stores in this city alone, I would no sooner touch that hair than I would a maggot-infested log of dog squat, until I had had the "hair" DNA tested to *prove,* scientifically, that every single short-and-curly on this weird machine was at least human and female in origin. And even then I'd be so uncomfortable and disturbed and just generally grossed out by the possible origins of the hair that arousal would be completely out of the question. And DNA testing be damned. I don't care if it is admissible in a court of law: Even the thought, the suspicion that somehow these could be male pubes would just defeat the purpose of the thing entirely for me. And as the sign states, "THERE ARE NO FUCKING RETURNS ON MERCHANDISE FOR ANY FUCK-ING REASON, SO DON'T EVEN FUCKING ASK!—THNX, THE MANAGEMENT." I think it's safe to assume that DNA testing falls under the category of "ANY FUCKING REASON," so never mind.

Besides, the "realistic" aspect of this vagina goes right out the window when the girl behind the Counter turns it on (as it were) and it begins to vibrate noisily in a most unromantic way, like a belt sander, and the insides of the thing can be seen to pulsate and constrict in strokes like a milking machine built for the cows of the Third Reich. Now, I'm no gynecologist (at least not licensed nor board certified), but I have been around the block once or twice, and around that block there have been strippers and belly dancers and teenage gymnasts, and I am telling you right now that this repugnant undulation is based in the same "reality" that Disney uses to find plots for its cartoons. Kegel can go piss up a rope: It just doesn't happen like that.

As the girl behind the Counter shoves the robotic twat back into its box (the possibilities for perverted sexuo-existential conundra are too numerous to choose from here), abject terror overtakes me as I realize that I am seconds away from being Next, and I have to ask this nubile and inked pincushion for a cock ring. To make matters nightmarishly worse, I am now noticing that there are many different species and sizes. There are metal ones, leather ones, rubber ones, ones that glow in the dark, ones that are studded like dog collars and have the word "bitch" on them in metal lettering. Other than that last one, which I know damn well I don't want anything to do with, I'm undecided.

And now I'm Next.

There are swarthy, sweating men with dubious criminal records behind me needing tokens.

The girl behind the Counter looks at me flatly. I have never seen anyone under 30 so completely jaded in my life. She says nothing—just stares at me the way one looks at vomit on the sidewalk outside a pub the morning after St. Patrick's Day. I stare up at her, exposing my throat in a way I'd rather not in present company.

"Um . . . I need—I mean I *want* . . . yes, I want to buy one of these . . ."

Did the doctor say metal? I think he said metal. Metal is stronger than leather or rubber. I want strength. I think the doctor said metal.

". . . um . . . one of these metal ones," I say, gesturing vaguely at the display case the same way Americans do when they order croissants when they know they can't even get close to proper pronunciation without sounding like a retarded call girl.

There are four sizes, and so, of course, she asks.

"What size?"

A brief flash of achievement and pride: I have just proved

size *does* in fact matter. I actually say it out loud before I can think it through.

"I guess size really *does* matter, heh heh."

"Bet your ass," she says with about as much enthusiasm and interest as I think will be mustered from her this week.

Swarthy parolees are shifting their weights audibly behind me and respirating with blatant impatience.

My pride at disproving the size-matters bullshit is shot to hell by the what-should-have-been-obviously-thought-through implication: I must now announce my size, which, as I've just made sure everybody in the place knows, matters very much.

The sizes appear to me to be small, medium, large, and extra large. I estimate my girth and make an educated guess. I am not boasting when I say that "small" is out of the question. The "small" ones are about the size of a quarter. And I'm not deluded enough to say that "extra large" is what is called for. Not even close. You could pass a grapefruit through these extra-larges with room to spare. So it's either medium or large. Of course I'd like to say "large," but I am both realistic and practical: The whole trick of the thing is to be snug, tight enough to constrict.

"Medium," I say, again pointing vaguely.

As anyone who speaks English and has ever tried to order a certain kind of doughnut from someone who doesn't speak English knows, this pointing-into-a-glass-case method of communication is right up there with midtornado smoke signals in terms of accuracy.

"This medium or this medium?" she asks, pointing at what I had considered medium and large.

I, self-esteem lying at my feet on the sticky floor like a with-ered but unused condom, point to the smaller of the two. I now am thankful for her jaded flatness. She doesn't act disappointed; she doesn't laugh or snicker; her expression remains as it has always been: uncaring to the point of complete detachment. She grabs the small medium (I guess that's better than a large small, but not much), drops it into a black plastic bag, punches some register buttons, and requests $12.50.

It's a metal ring. It cost about seven cents to make. But, $12.50. This better work.

Something told me that initial experiments with the c-ring should be conducted alone, in secure privacy. And so it was.

The doctor said that you slip the ring around the thing, and as the thing becomes "engorged" (There is something about that word that bugs the hell out of me; I can't quite pin it down, though), the ring constricts the thing and prevents blood from flowing back out. Sounds simple enough.

So, here we go.

Whoo! The ring is *cold* on the thing. Hold the ring in the palm of a clenched hand for a few seconds to achieve accept-able temperature. There. Okay.

The ring is around the thing and after mild manual agita-tion, the thing becomes the King.

Well, hot damn—look at that. He's baaaack.

But, uh . . . hmmm. It's definitely working. Blood flow is most definitely being constricted. The ring is snug around the King, *tight*, even.

Okay, yeah . . . we're now overachieving here. The King's

crown, if you will, and slowly, the entire King itself, is turning an alarming shade of blue.

I try to remove the thing from the King, but it won't budge. It's like the goddamn sword in the stone. Attempts at forced budging only painfully exacerbate the situation. *Ouch!* Bad move. This is not good. Okay . . . think . . . soap and warm water.

Naked, I stand to walk to the bathroom, and my unit bounces. And it hurts. A lot. Okay . . . must hold it while moving—movement hurts.

I carefully and nimbly walk down the hall toward the bathroom in the same way people walk seconds after their laxatives kick in: hurried, but careful . . . quick travel with a minimum of motion.

Despite the pain, the manual application of warm soapy water does nothing to curb the hyperstimulation factor here. In fact, it is only making it worse. And the ring won't budge.

Okay . . . think harder. No! *Softer! Think softer.*

Cold shower.

Cold showers are to me what sunlight is to vampires: painful, cringe- and anger-inducing brutality that causes me to recoil and retreat. I hate them. But in lieu of any other idea, in I go.

My neighbors, who have left malicious and threatening notes on my door wishing me cancer or worse, who have stopped me in the hall to tell me that they pray nightly for my early death or eviction, are used to unusual noises coming from within these walls. But not even I was prepared for the barbaric howl I let loose from under the steady pressure of the bitterly cold water. After a few seconds, I assumed an awkward position that, in any other circumstance, might look like advanced Tai Chi or performance art, desperately trying to ensure that only what needed to be sprayed with cold water was only what was being sprayed with cold water.

No dice. The pressure of the water added even more pain to an already excruciating situation, and the temperature caused the blueness to deepen alarmingly: We're talking *mauve*.

Something in my subconscious, someplace waaaaay down in the deep animal-survival regions, sent up an alarm that somehow said clearly without using words: Black means dead. If this thing turns black, they are going to have to amputate. Isn't that the case with tourniquets? What about frostbite? So what the hell am I doing in a freezing cold shower?

In my panicked state, the idea actually passes through my head to somehow utilize the microwave. I've never understood how a microwave really works, but maybe somehow . . .

No. Can't put metal in a microwave.

Metal! Who gives a shit about metal! I'm actually thinking about putting my penis into a microwave oven! This isn't a folded bag of freeze-dried popcorn . . . it's my dick, for fuck's sake!

Clearly, I had gone beyond my own limitations and judgment and experience and was in over my head in the worst way. No choice. Call the doctor.

Because it is "after hours," I am automatically patched through to the doctor's generic answering service.

"Doctor's Office."

"I need to speak to Dr. _____."

"This is his answering service. Is this an emergency?"

"Pretty much, yeah."

"For medical emergencies, you should dial 911 immediately."

"I'd rather not. I'd rather just speak with the doctor directly. Now."

"I can page him for you, but there's no telling how long it will take or even *if* he'll respond tonight. If this is a medical emergency, I highly recommend you dial 911."

"Look. What's your name?"

"Jerome."

"Okay, Jerome. Listen. This *is* a medical emergency, but it's not life-threatening. But it *is* plenty fucking threatening in a very personal sort of way, and I think a straightforward conversation with the doctor is probably all that is needed. Please just page the doctor now."

Jerome is thinking. "Okay, Let me get your name."

"This is Jayson Gallaway."

"And what is the emergency?"

"That's between me and the doctor."

Jerome is thinking even harder now. "Mr. Gallaway, I *have* to tell the doctor what this is concerning when I page him."

"Just tell him my name. He'll understand."

"I'm sorry, Mr. Gallaway; the doctor is at the annual Fondue and Awards Dinner for his fly-fishing club, and he left really specific instructions about being disturbed."

I glance down. I close my eyes. I can't bear to look. I've gone completely numb in a part that was designed to feel. Even my nerve endings are losing hope. And did he just say "fondue"? Fuck it.

"Tell the doctor my penis is almost completely black."

Jerome thinks a second, and then starts *chuckling*. "Well, yeah, brother, so is mine . . . that's no emergency. It's all good."

"It sure as shit *is* an emergency, my brother, and it's all bad. The rest of me is the way it's been since I was born: white as a sheet. Now page the goddamn doctor!"

"Oh shit . . . I mean, I'm sorry, I'll page him right away. And, there's no need to bring up any white sheets. What's your phone number?"

"He has it. Thank you, Jerome."

Three minutes later, my phone rings.

"Hello?"

"Your dick is black?"

"Damn near."

"What the hell did you do?"

"I did exactly what you told me to do, quack."

"No need to be hostile."

"There is a very big, swollen, dark reason for me to be hostile currently protruding from my crotch."

"What do you . . . oh wait . . . did you get a cock ring?"

"Just like you told me to."

"What kind? Leather?"

"Metal. You told me metal."

"I never told you metal."

"I swear you said 'metal.' "

"I can assure you I never specifically told you to get a metal cock ring."

"Whatever. We'll deal with that in court. Right now, we need to deal with what we need to deal with right now."

"Is there pain?"

"You moron! What do you think? Damn right there's pain. At least there was. Extreme pain. But now it's . . . numb."

"Numb? How long has it been numb?"

"I don't know. Four minutes. Maybe ten. Shit, I'm not sitting here staring at the clock. Besides, time is doing funny things. I feel dizzy."

"Are you sitting down?"

"No."

"Sit down. How are your testicles?"

"Fine. Great. The usual. But they're worried. They're worried just like America would be worried if all of Canada suddenly turned black."

"You may be going into shock. I want you take slow, deep breaths."

"I'm going to sue you."

"Yes, you're definitely going into shock. Now help me understand, because this isn't adding up. You got a metal cock ring and you put it around your penis and your testicles?"

"Just my penis."

A pause. A pause that would be described as "pregnant" by anyone without a dangerously darkening numb member that looks as if it has been burned and frostbitten.

"Shit," he says, his tone still somehow completely professional. This can't be good.

Silence.

"What do you mean, 'Shit'? 'Shit' what?"

"Well, you're not supposed to just put it around your penis . . . it's supposed to go around your entire genitalia: penis, testicles, the works."

"Oh shit."

"Exactly."

"So what the fuck do I do?"

"How tight is the ring?"

"I can only see the sides of it. If my unit were a fat man and

the ring were a belt, fat would be hanging over it on all sides
and kids at the mall would make fun of him."

"Oh shit."

"Quit saying that!"

"You said it, too. Why can't I say it?"

"Forget it. What do I need to do?"

"You *have* to go to the emergency room."

"Which one?"

"Doesn't matter."

"Yes it does."

"Why?"

"Because you have to meet me there."

"What?"

"There is no fucking way I am going to go trudging,
pigeon-toed, into any public place and tell some total stranger
that I was conducting experiments on my own penis, and I
apparently underestimated my own girth and potential for
growth, and now the once-mighty Ivory Tower looks like a
withered 73-year-old black man from Alabama named Ordell
who has gone more than a week without any pork and has
taken to eating cigarettes. Where do you want to meet me?"

"Jayson, the people at the ER are used to stuff a *lot* weirder
than this."

"Good for them. I don't give a shit. A black penis erupting
from a white torso is about as weird as it gets for me. Do you
want me to come pick you up?"

"You need to go to the hospital *right now!* Every second you
spend bullshitting with me is one more second closer to . . .
cut-off time."

I could tell he had chosen his words carefully.

"Bullshitting? Is that what we're doing here, Doc? Just a couple of fellas shooting the shit? You think I'm *bullshitting?* Listen . . . this is your fault, and not only will I litigate like a bitter pit bull, but someday, somehow, sooner that you think, I'm going to write a book and in this book I shall lampoon you with impunity, and denounce you before God and the entire world as a charlatan, a quack, and an unfeeling, inhumane bastard who sat around eating fondue and pork tartare with his fly-fishing buddies while one of his patients' cock was turning into a retiree named Ordell before falling off."

"How the hell do you know where I am?"

"Jerome told me. He's an idiot. You need to get a new service."

"He *is* an idiot, but at least his penis is the same color it was when he woke up this morning."

Just then a rogue wave of pain from the sea of numbness hit me and silenced any retort, allowing me only to moan in agony.

"All right, Jayson, go to St. Francis right now, and I'll meet you there as soon as I can. I'll leave now, okay?"

"Mrrrrrrrmb."

"Can you make it?"

"Mrrrrrrrmb."

"Okay, now I'll meet you there and treat you, but you still need to be admitted, so get started filling out the forms and tell the admitting nurse that I'm on my way to meet you, okay?"

"Mrrrrrrrmb."

I should not have driven, but there was no way I could have artfully dealt with any sort of taxi, and an ambulance was out of the question. At least it was when I left my apartment. But once on the road, it was very much back in the question as I approached what would be the first of many stop lights: The pain caused by exerting pressure on the brake pedal caused me dizziness and made my vision grow dark. Accelerating wasn't exactly pleasant either, but it wasn't as bad. And that, combined with my ever-increasing desire to get to the hospital, was sufficient cause for me to begin blowing through lights as if they were Christmas decorations. California Street is simply littered with stoplights, and each one seemed to sense my approach and would turn a brief yellow and then a harsh shade of "fuck you" red. It was probably Jesus getting back at me for calling him a hippie (see "Hindsight on 20/20"). Screw it, I thought. Mr. Turn-the-Other-Cheek can play Turn-Another-Stop-Light if He wants to, but my agenda was now more important. Sure, he had been crucified and crowned with thorns and speared in the side, but not even He would have tolerated wang strangulation. Nor will I.

Somehow I make it to the hospital, park illegally on the sidewalk, and trudge, as pigeon-toed and pathetic as predicted, into the emergency room. It takes all of my strength to tell the admitting nurse through viciously gritted teeth that my doctor will be meeting me here shortly, and he told me he would handle everything, and I should just get started on the paperwork, and can I please just have the paperwork now, please; thank you. She eyes me with blatant faithlessness but hands over the prearranged clipboard holding the usual forms.

Within minutes, my doctor sweeps in, his white doctor's coat over a casual suit, takes the clipboard from me, helps me up, waves knowingly to the admitting nurse and security guard

(Where did the guard come from? He wasn't there before. Had that suspicious nurse called him?), and leads me into the ER proper. In my woozy condition, I barely remember a brief conversation between him and the attending physician. It is a thankfully slow night at St. Francis, and there is a private room available.

"Go ahead and take off your pants," says the doctor calmly as he puts on a pair of latex gloves. Combat boots, socks, and pants hit the floor in quick succession, and grasping poor withered Ordell, I carefully collapse onto the gurney/bed.

"Ho, Jesus Christ!" he exclaims when he turns around. "We don't have much time." I wonder if this guy really does have a medical license or if he just watches a lot of TV.

He squirts half a tube of K-Y jelly onto one gloved hand, making a sound that would cause me to cackle adolescently under any other circumstance. He picks up my dying member gently, but not gently enough and I almost pass out. In fact, I *try* to pass out. In keeping with the theme of the evening, I fail. He liberally applies the other half of the tube of lubricant to Ordell. I feel like I'm on the set of the most ill-conceived gay porn ever made. When he manipulates the ring at all, when he in any way even acknowledges the presence of the ring, I writhe in agony, further irritating Ordell, further exasperating the doctor. He looks at me calmly and says the best words I've heard in recent memory: "You need some drugs." Amen, brother.

My doctor leaves the room. I pray to every deity of which I have ever heard. I make a few up and pray to them, too. I watch the oversized clock on the wall. He is gone four minutes. Soon, he returns with a female, a nurse, in tow. She gasps. Audibly. Like the nurse in *The Elephant Man* who, despite the doctor's warnings, can't help herself. I don't care. She looks into my eyes and smiles. "Hi, I'm Suzy." I rictus in return.

"Yeah, we actually get quite a few of these," she says to the doctor. She sinks an IV needle into my arm. And though it does hurt like a bastard, I welcome the pain: *Anything* to distract me from what's going on down south. In a moment, I become very alarmed when it occurs to me that my veins are being tapped, but I have surrendered. These are professionals. Whatever they have to do is fine with me. I have lost my fight.

As she is setting up the IV, she and my doctor have an intense and cryptic discussion of which I understand practically nothing, other than they are going to intravenously administer 8 mgs. of morphine and 1 mg. of Ativan, which, again, sounds fine to me. They use terms like "priapism" and "penile incarceration." *Shit . . . am I going to go to jail for this little stunt? Have they written "5150" on my chart? Is that why I got a private room? Am I a risk to myself or others? Penile incarceration? Are they going to send me to a penile colony, like a leper colony, where I will live out the rest of my meaninglessly suffering days in some weird, impoverished Third World village with a bunch of other hopeless, depressed, automatonic zombies with necrotic cocks dangling lifelessly from their skinny torsos as they wander about aimlessly, or sit, unmoving, in withdrawn states of permanent shock?*

"First, we'll wrap the penis tightly from the tip to the base to try to reduce the swelling."

"Ice pack?" asks my doctor. I shoot him a look and imagine what his head would look like on a stick. Luckily, the nurse vetoes his idea immediately.

"Direct substantial pressure will reduce the swelling as well as ice in this case; ice will just be unnecessarily painful."

Yeah . . . eat it, Doctor Dipshit. The nurse knows more than you, you sadistic Nazi.

I want to give my doctor the finger, but I still am seriously concerned about the possibility that he could have me sent to a penile colony: He's obviously pretty pissed about my threat of legal action and the interruption of his fondue.

Note to self: If this works, dedicate life to having this nurse canonized: She is a saint. Saint Suzy. If Ordell ever works again, I will name my first child Suzy. Even if it's a boy.

My doctor fiddles with the IV, loading the thing up with morphine and Ativan and other things that happy boys are made of. And the pain ebbs away slowly, gently . . . almost like a fading sound . . . going . . . going . . . and who cares. Not I. I now am floating on a cloud of intravenously administered bliss. My jaw, as well as the muscles in my neck, shoulders, and back, all of which have been clenched together tightly for the last hour or so, miraculously relax. Everything is going to be fine. Everything *is* fine.

Then I vomit all over myself and Saint Suzy. Everyone seems to take this in stride, especially me. *I am in a wonderful mood.* Now Saint Suzy is cradling Ordell gently and, with great care, engulfing him tightly in a rather pleasant cotton wrap. Saint Suzy is very good with her hands. Saint Suzy is rather attractive. Perhaps I should propose to her. I might if I had a ring. *Oh but I do have a ring:* She just has to remove it from the base of my once and future King. Mmmm . . . yes, she will successfully remove the ring, restore Ordell to his former glory, and to reward her, I shall propose to Saint Suzy. And she will surely say yes, for how could any woman resist an invitation to spend the rest of forever with a guy she met in the ER, who wandered in

one night with a constricted piece of turkey jerky where the
Penis Formerly Known as the King used to reside, whose vomit
still is dripping from her hands as she quickly goes to the sink to
rinse off.

She gets to the base where her soon-to-be-engagement ring
is currently on display, and fastens the bandage tightly. She then
liberally coats the inside of one finger of a latex glove with lube
and deftly slips the finger of the glove over the now-cotton-
engulfed Ordell. It takes some effort and sustained pressure,
and it looks like it should hurt, but I don't feel a damn thing. In
fact, I am feeling so good about things that I can now watch the
goings-on at the South Pole with removed interest, like a
passerby at the scene of a traffic accident. It's almost funny: It
looks like a little mummy.

Wait a minute! That's not funny! They're mummifying Ordell!
He is dead and they are preserving him for display in some
future museum of medicinal idiocy! Centuries from now, children on field trips will file past the mummified remains of my
dismembered member, and gaze in horrified awe and disbelief.
Little girls will playfully scream and cover their mouths and
turn away, laughing in mock disgust. The preteen boys will be
quiet, wanting to joke, but finding themselves silenced by
something inside that they don't yet understand, whispering
into their subconsciouses the warning of St. Augustine: "There,
but for the grace of God, go I."

Amen, brother. Amen indeed.

No. Too negative. I feel great. Everything is going to be fine.
No museum. No kids. No mummy wangs. I decide to shoot the
shit with my doctor.

"Sorry about the fondue," I say, and I mean it. To interrupt a man's fondue dipping for *any* reason is an unconscionable breach of etiquette in any civilized culture.

"No worries," he says. I get the impression he is not in the mood to talk. He's always been a bit uptight. High strung. He needs to relax more, and I'm not thinking that just because I'm high as a pine on morphine. It would be good for his bedside manner. Perhaps he could just run another tube from this IV and hook himself up. We could bond over pharmaceuticals . . . bridge the gap that's always prevented us from being actual friends. I wonder if I can get one of these IV things to go. Get a traveler for the road. Such an acquisition could greatly improve my quality of life, my tolerance of others. I actually could become a "good person." Really, this morphine is ter-rific. Everybody makes a big deal out of the discovery of peni-cillin. Shit. I'm allergic to penicillin. Fuck penicillin. And that guy who cured polio. Fuck him. Morphine could kick Jonas Salk's ass. What was that other stuff they put in there? Ativan?

"Hey, Doc?"

"Yes, Jayson?"

"I'm really sorry about the fondue. I mean sincerely, that was fucked up, what I said about suing you and stuff."

"I know, Jayson. Don't worry. It's fine."

"I haven't had fondue in a fuckin' decade."

"It's good stuff."

"Fuckin' A. The *best*." My eyes close in fond recollection. "Fon-fuckin'-due."

The doctor says nothing.

"Hey, Doc?"

"Yes, Jayson?"

"What's Ativan?"

"It's something to help you relax. It helps with anxiety."

"I don't have any anxiety."

"Exactly."

"BAH-Haahaahaahaaa!"

The doctor is startled by my outburst of laughter.

"Yeah, Doc, you are one funny motherfucker. 'Exactly.' That was great. Yeah."

Whoa . . . I almost faded there for a second. It would be so easy to just drift off now . . . float away on this opiated cloud into the welcoming arms of Morpheus. But no . . . I need to stay here, stay awake, see what's happening . . . what we are doing.

"Hey, Doc?"

"Yes, Jayson?"

"What are we doing?"

"We're waiting for Suzy."

"Yeah. She's nice, isn't she?"

"Yes she is."

"Cute, too."

"I suppose so."

"Oh, c'mon, Doc . . . lighten up . . . she's cute. Say it."

"Sure . . . she's cute."

"Bet your ass."

Silence.

"Doc?"

"Yo."

"What's Suzy doing?"

"She's waiting for the fire department to get here."

"No shit. Huh. That's really something. Shit. Is the hospital on fire? Should we be leaving? I'll need another one of these IVs to take with me."

"There's no fire. Everything's fine. We'll just wait right here."

"Cool. Is that oxygen in that tank right there?"

"That's right. Good old O^2."

"Can you hook that mask up real quick so I can get a toot off it? Might help me relax—straighten out a bit."

"Maybe later."

"Cool."

I nod off for I don't know how long. I wake up feeling well rested: terrific. I'm in the same room. The doctor still is here. Saint Suzy still is gone.

"Doc?"

"Right here."

"How long did I sleep?"

"Mmm . . . ten, maybe fifteen seconds."

"You're shittin' me."

"I'm crapping you negative, big guy."

"Morphine is nice."

"That's the rumor."

"So why's the fire department coming? Can't someone else wait for the fire department? I miss Suzy."

A pause. *Fuck it. Who cares?* I drift off again. *Nice.*

Wait a minute.

"Doc?"

"What is it?"

"Why is Suzy waiting for the fire department?"

He sighs. "Well, your problem is actually pretty common in San Francisco . . . so much so that the fire department here actually has a special tool they use to fix your . . . situation."

"Good to know . . . good to know. Pretty common in San Francisco, you said?"

"Happens all the time."

"It's a gay thing, isn't it, Doc?"

"That's not at all true."

"So this is common in, like, Kansas? Ya think the ol' FD down in Laredo, Texas, has a 'special tool'?"

"Now calm down, Jayson . . . don't get upset."

"You told me cock rings weren't a gay thing. I asked you and you said no."

"They're not a 'gay' thing."

"Bongwash. Give me my pants."

"Why do you need your pants?"

"Because my phone is in them."

"Why do you need your phone?"

"Because I am going to call Las Cruces, New Mexico, and I'm going to ask to speak to the mayor, and I'm going to ask him if the LCFD has a special fucking tool for the removal of stuck cock rings, and I am going to put you on the phone and I want you listen to what I'll bet a testicle is *cackling* laughter."

"Jayson, lie back down; you're going to pull out your IV."

"Oooh . . . bad. Thanks, Doc. Wouldn't want that." I lie back down. When I get out of here, I'm going to look online for one of these morphine-drip devices. Check out eBay. I am so much more agreeable and patient. I really am a good person.

I nod off again. I have vivid and lengthy dreams about Xanadu, and a stately pleasure dome where I am king. Huge bolts of lavish silk are draped from the ceiling and walls. The floor is covered in Persian rugs, harem pillows, and hookahs. My favorite porn starlet, a girl named Friday, lounges languidly and slowly strokes a tiger kitten I have given her as a reward for last night's performance. There are caged nymphettes with veils undulating constantly to Ravel's *Bolero*. Some of them who are not encaged fan Friday with carefully crafted collections of ornate peacock feathers. Next to the golden throne upon which I sit, Joan Jett strokes my hair and attends to the royal morphine drip. Joan, who clearly is in charge of the ladies, suggests that we all go for a bath in the royal pool. The girls squeal with excitement and bounce toward the small heated pool at the base of the steps to the throne. All of the girls walk or run on their toes, like cats. I am the last into the pool. The water is fine.

And then I come around (as in wake up). Nobody here except my ugly-ass doctor.

"How long that time?"

"About five seconds."

"Amazing. I had this dream I was Chaka Khan."

"Chaka Khan . . . the soul singer? You dreamed you were a fat black woman?"

"No . . . not Chaka . . . it was a guy. Did Chaka have a brother?"

"I have no idea."

"No . . . come on, Doc . . . this was the greatest dream ever . . . I was a guy . . . Genghis Khan? I decreed a stately pleasure dome."

"Kubla Khan?"

"*Disco*. I was Kubla Khan, and Joan Jett was there, and Friday."

"What happens on Friday?"

"I'll tell you what happens on Friday. First she does this dance with seven veils, and then . . ."

"I get the idea."

"I wanna be Kubla Khan."

"You do have the characteristics of a Mongoloid."

Opiates or not . . . I think I've been insulted. Royal umbrage is taken. This will not stand: "What the fuck do you mean by that?"

"Mongoloid . . . of or pertaining to the Mongol hordes. You know . . . fearsome warriors. Like Kubla and Genghis. And Chaka."

"Damn right. Fearsome warrior. If I go back to sleep, will you tell Suzy that I am a fearsome warrior?"

"I will definitely tell her you are a Mongoloid, but I think she has her own suspicions."

"Yeah. Probably. Hey! *There* she is!"

In walks Saint Suzy, smiling, but grimly somehow. She holds the door open for . . . one, two, three, four, FIVE! Five fucking firemen! (In my opiated psyche, Count von Count from Sesame Street speaks in a corny Transylvanian accent: "FIVE! Five Fucking Firemen—ah, ah, ah, ahhhhh!")

"What the hell is this?" No one answers me, so I'm left to my own narcotized powers of observation. Five guys. Five. Firefighters. With oversized helmets, huge asbestos coats, badges, big stompy boots. The room is now so crowded that the fifth guy can only get his left half in. I look at my doctor the way people look at things they are about to kill.

"I thought you said the building wasn't on fire."

"It's not." I've never heard him sound sheepish before, and it doesn't escape me that he just took a step back from the bedside, just out of striking distance.

The cloud of tranquility and contentment upon which I've

been adrift for who cares how long suddenly dissipates and sends me crashing ass-over-teakettle toward the unforgiving asphalt of reality.

"If the building is not on fire, perhaps you can explain to me why half the goddamn battalion is standing around my bed in full gear. Do you realize I am not wearing pants?"

My doctor is not even looking at me anymore. I turn to the brigade of fire guys. I don't care that I'm not wearing pants. I'm pissed off.

"Why didn't you guys go all out and bring the hook and ladder around the side of the building and come crashing through the window?" Their collective silence and lack of reaction is completely unnerving. Less than two minutes ago, I was in a Pleasure Dome with Friday, and now I'm in a nightmare with Engine 666.

The humiliation of lying in a hospital bed wearing nothing but a t-shirt that says, "I Spit on Your Dress Code" with a mummified schlong while surrounded by six (5.5 since that last guy still is only halfway in the room) men and one attractive even-when-besplattered-with-vomit female, all of whom, it is more than worth noting, not only adhere to dress codes, but wear fucking *uniforms,* is about as bad as it gets. At least they didn't bring one of those big fuck-off axes they use to chop down doors. Yes. Things could be worse.

Or so I thought.

Then I found out why the right half of the last guy had been left outside the room. I saw the bolt cutters.

"Fuck *YOU!*" I yelled at the bolt cutters and the fire brigade and everyone in the room and all practitioners of Western medicine who can successfully treat neuroblastomas in utero with lasers, but when it comes to Jayson's penis, the best that modern medical technology and the greatest minds in medicochirurgical science have to offer is a call to the fire station to bring down a fucking pair of bolt cutters. I'm outta here.

"Fuck you all, and those big-ass bolt cutters, too!"

"We're going to need two more mgs. of Ativan," my doctor yells.

"No, you're gonna need about 1,000 mgs. of Ativan and some pepper spray and a goddamn shotgun, because if you think I'm letting that son of a bitch anywhere *near* Ordell, with that big fucking bolt cutter, fuck you. It's my *penis,* you moron . . . it's not a deadbolt!"

Everyone begins moving, jockeying for positions.

"I'll fight every one of you cocksmoking hose boys! Doc, gimme my pants. C'mon Ordell . . . we're leaving."

The firefighter with the bolt cutters gets a look on his face like someone just wiped dogshit on his mustache: "Who's Ordell?" he asks.

"Ordell is my wang, and I'm his bodyguard. Take one step toward me with those bolt cutters and I swear to Christ you'll take the rest of your meals through a straw. *Doc, give me my goddamn pants!* Quit dicking around with that stupid IV. Doc! Hey Doc! Well, fuck you, too, then, you ignorant schmuck. I have rights. I have a legal right to have my pants. *I demand you give me my pants!*"

When I come to, it is abruptly, as if my consciousness is controlled by a light switch that someone just flipped on. I am in a different room. No firefighters. No doctor. No Saint Suzy. *Saint Suzy.* Hah. She's the one who called the SFFD about my c-ring. That *Judas!* That mendacious slut whore. And to think I was going to marry someone like that. She's probably just hot for one of the fire guys and used Ordell as an excuse to . . .

Wait . . . Ordell.

Whoa . . . bad idea trying to lift the old cranium. Whatever is in the IV still is running strong. I think I'll let my fingers do the walking. And . . . *Eureka!* Ordell is still in the house. His latex-glove finger is gone, and he is no longer wrapped tightly, but bandaged softly and loosely. And yes . . . that awful goddamn ring is gone, too.

I sigh with relief and smile: happy day; happy day. The sun will come up tomorrow. Won't it? Can I be sure? I need more info. I press the button that summons the nurse. I am still very heavy-lidded, still faded. When no one comes in what feels like a reasonable amount of time (about 10 seconds), I hit the button again. Soon, the door opens. It is *Her.* Suzy. The Whore of the Ring.

She smiles sincerely: "You're awake."

"Barely."

"How are you feeling?"

"That depends."

"On?"

"The prognosis."

She pulls up a chair but is still smiling, so I'm hoping the news isn't dire.

"Well, we were able to remove the ring . . ."

I don't ask if it was with the bolt cutters . . . I don't want to know.

". . . and now we'll just have to wait and see. In a few days, we'll be able to tell how much, if any, tissue necrotized. Depending on that, you may need some corrective cosmetic surgery."

I'm not sure I am hearing her correctly through the drug fog: "Did you say *cosmetic surgery? On the wang?*"

She laughs. "Maybe. It happens more than you'd think. It's called balanoplasty. Your damaged tissue could appear . . . *fluffy* I guess is the only way to describe it."

I have to laugh. In the space of, I don't know . . . six, maybe seven hours, my penis has changed from the Mighty Ivory Tower to an emaciated black man named Ordell, and has somehow emerged as a potential deformity known only as "Fluffy."

Suzy sees the furrow of my brow and senses my worry. "Don't worry . . . it's very minor work . . . it won't end up looking like Michael Jackson or anything."

She means to humor me, but that actually really does make me feel better. It's bad enough to have Ordell or Fluffy to deal with, but seeing Michael Jackson between one's thighs is something found only in the Eighth Circle of Hell, a punishment reserved only for the most egregious pedophiles.

Two hours later, Suzy and the attending physician release me, and after I awkwardly thank her, she calls another nurse who helps me into a wheelchair to take me to the front door of the hospital.

"One more thing I forgot to mention . . ." says Suzy, causing the nurse to stop pushing and turn the chair around so I can see Saint Suzy one last time.

"I'd avoid the Viagra, at least for a while. That could really complicate things."

"Where did *that* come from?" I ask, looking at her as if she'd just reminded me to take my birth-control pills.

"I saw you on TV . . . I was trying all night to figure out where I'd seen you. Your doctor told me about it, and that's when I put it together."

Fuck a duck.

POSTSCRIPT

I spent the next five days in a Darvocet stupor, watching PBS in between episodes of blissful drug-induced unconsciousness, PBS being the only thing on TV guaranteed not to make me laugh, laughter being an agonizing occurrence during recovery from this particular injury. As was sneezing. Thankfully I sneezed only once during those five days, but it was something that I will never forget. I couldn't even officially finish the sneeze. I just dropped to my knees and punched a hole straight through the drywall of my living room, right through to my bedroom.

The only other event of note came the morning after I was released from the hospital: It was when I had to pee.

Let us pause for a moment to understand the depth of terror this proposition instilled in my soul. How to explain it? One time I tried to climb a hill which, as I climbed higher and higher, turned into a cliff. About halfway up the cliff, I realized I could go neither up nor down, and was stuck there until I let go and fell or got pulled to safety. Another time, I had someone without a badge or any sort of constituted authority point a loaded gun at my face. The feelings these events induced were *nothing* compared to the dread and doom I felt as I stood before the bowl that morning.

Surprisingly, it brought no additional pain to the constant ache that I was just beginning to get used to. But when I went, it . . . *sputtered,* like when you turn on a hose that hasn't been turned on for a while: Some liquid, the air, causing an absolutely surreal farting sound that you'd expect to find in a Burroughs's book, and a feeling that, though not unpleasant, was just undeniably *wrong.*

Within a week, things had pretty much returned to normal. Coloring, texture, functionality . . . and on the eighth day: pain-less morning wood.

The Ivory Tower stood proud. I actually saluted and hummed "The Star Spangled Banner." I even improvised new words: "Oh say does that once strangled member still stand . . . when there are girls, it is free, and when alone, for the hand." Or something like that.

Oh hey . . . don't tell anybody about that "Fluffy" bullshit or I won't share any of my leftover Darvocet with you.

Burning Man—The Big BM

I started getting mail from around the world about the Viagra story, and a lot of that mail was from editors of publications offering me work. "Why not?" I thought. Most of the ideas they had were interesting, if not downright bizarre, and though the pay was not glorious, it had to be more rewarding than the graveyard shift at Kinko's.

My terms at that point were simple: I'll take any assignment you throw at me, as long as it has nothing to do with Viagra or my penis. The terms of the first assignment I was offered were simple: Drive to the middle of the Nevada desert and check out something called Burning Man, and report back.

Other than not really wanting to go to Burning Man, I had no problem with the job: $400 cash up front for initial expenses, reimbursement of additional expenses upon return, and then a grand or so for the story. But the tone of this San Francisco–based magazine surprised me: They seemed to have absolutely no clue what Burning Man was. I also was a bit surprised when I showed up to pick up my stipend at the magazine's offices, a huge office/loft space that was fully furnished for a staff of 100 or so, but only 3 people occupied the place. It was obvious this once-mighty organization had gone through about 12 rounds of layoffs, and I suddenly was afraid this $400 was all I was ever going to see for my troubles. Because I was vicariously quite knowledgeable about Burning Man (various friends had been trying to convince me to go to this thing for nearly a decade, always using glorious stories and pictures of naked people from the previous year as bait), I started thinking of ways to write the story without having to blow this envelope of cash on the supplies and general hassle of actually going to the event. I chatted briefly with the assignment editor, who, from the moment I saw him, struck me as somehow indefinably satanic. Perhaps it was the goatee. Maybe the black fingernails. I couldn't place it. But for this and many other reasons that shall become clear soon, let's call him the Antichrist.

Jayson: I got the impression from our phone conversation that I'm supposed to write this thing from the perspective of someone who has never even heard of Burning Man . . . is that true?

Antichrist: Yeah . . . someone mentioned it at a meeting and it sounded like something we'd be interested in.

Jayson: How so? I mean, what's the angle?

Antichrist: Well, no one here has actually gone, but it sounds like a bunch of naked people running around on drugs and lighting things on fire, ya know . . . stoned naked girls blowing things up . . . that sort of thing. That's the angle. Youthful recreation in the 21st century.

Jayson: I think I can do that story, but I'm not sure I actually need to go there to do it. Don't get me wrong . . . I'm big on drugs, naked chicks, and explosions . . . shit, nobody's bigger. But, if you just want a sort-of general societal scoop, I know a bit about Burning Man: I could just pound it out and have it to you in a couple of days.

Antichrist: Oh no, absolutely not. We need to have a first-hand account of the events of this year. We want gory details, like you did with that Diary of a . . .

Jayson [interrupting]: Yeah, I understand. Sure. Okay. I'll do it.

The editor rose from his chair and stepped around the side of his desk to shake on it. I couldn't help but notice he was barefoot. He grinned eerily: "You should be happier, dude . . . you're getting paid to take a vacation and write about it. It'll rock."

As I rode the bus back to my apartment, I felt uneasy: a small cash advance, promises of reimbursement and bigger money later, no written contract, all from a spooky guy with no shoes in an office with no staff. And he had called me "dude."

But, it was high time for a vacation, even if the "vacation" was being sent out into the middle of a desert by the editorial Antichrist. On the other hand, I could think of at least 100 things I'd rather do with this grip of cash than fund a hippie desert holiday.

I spent that night surfing the innumerable Web sites and stories and pictures of the ghosts of Burning Men past. I started churning out prose, thinking, somehow, someway, I could pull it off without driving out into the weird Nevada moonscape and getting dirty. But, it wasn't happening. It bugged me ethically, sure, but I sensed early on that this editor wasn't too concerned about ethics. In the end, it was the realization that I can't just make up the sort of weirdness that happens at things like this. I'd have to go and see things for myself.

And so I did.

It was not a vacation . . . . it was penance. It was punishment for things I didn't even know I had done, or maybe things I hadn't done yet. The results, I think, speak for themselves. To wit:

Some background

The annual event known as Burning Man is held in the Black Rock Desert of Nevada and has gone from something incredibly and atavistically cool to something almost purposefully identical to the precise thing it was created to escape. So far this year, there have been more than 30,000 advance tickets sold and several hundred "theme camps" "licensed" by the organizers of El Hombre en Fuego.

Though defying any normal categorization, Burning Man is best perceived as a performance-art festival on steroids. And acid. And mescaline. And mushrooms. And most of all, *on fire*. Every year, tens of thousands of people (always several thousand more than the previous year) journey to the Black Rock Desert, camp under ferocious conditions (think Mars with *slightly* better weather), and either set up or perform "art" of boundless genres. The event derives its name from the included effigy of a man (essentially a giant stick figure with a triangulated head) made out of wood and neon, and absolutely packed with incendiary and pyrotechnic devices. All of the performances and art installations and whatever come to a crescendo on the "night of the Burn," when the tens of thousands of attendees gather in full costume (or complete nudity) around this five-story flammable erection (!) and dance around in a scene disturbingly similar to the Cambodian natives dancing at the end of *Apocalypse Now*, only, instead of sacrificially killing a water buffalo, they set the Man on fire and (due to the explosives that have been packed into the framework of the thing) blow the shit out of it.

Because this is what Hakim Bey would call a "Temporary Autonomous Zone," certain conventions, like clothing, go (often literally and horribly) out the proverbial window. It is a spectacle unlike any other on the planet, and is so full of material for sociological and behavioral psychological theses and dissertations that the mind completely reels.

But despite its anarchic reputation, the event is a hyperorganized symphony of planning.

The whole thing was conceived and still is run (to some extent) by Larry Harvey, an adopted child from the outskirts of Portland, Oregon, who grew up feeling lonely and isolated. Of his childhood home, Harvey says, "We were on top of thirty feet of loam. We had chickens."

But as Burning Man has grown exponentially over its 17-year history, administration of the ritual/event has necessarily grown proportionally. It now is run as a municipality, albeit a temporary one, with a sort-of city council, police force (called the Danger Rangers), medical services and facilities, daily newspapers, radio stations, and postal service.

A brief history and explanation of the evolution (and subtextual hints of the devolution) of Burning Man (tied in with a segue into an exploration of how I eventually ended up in that godforsaken desert high as a giraffe's

ass on 'shrooms wondering if anyone had seen my pants)

Okay, so as mentioned above, once upon a time there was a man named Larry Harvey. Legend has it that Larry had a particularly bad year in 1986 (girlfriend dumped him, yadda yadda yadda), and so Larry decided he would take a dozen or so friends out to Baker Beach in San Francisco during the Summer Solstice and construct an improvised eight-foot wooden figure, and everyone would mentally project all of their bad feelings and negative energy and so on onto this thing and set that fucker on fire in a sort-of spontaneous pagan bacchanalian orgiastic exorcism. And so it was. And as the thing went up in flames, bystanders came cruising over and started dancing around, and boy, isn't this a great idea and why don't we do it again next year?

So, 1987 rolls around, and the original attendees bring a few of their friends who bring a few of their friends out to Baker Beach and build a 20-foot Man and light it on fire and dance around and have a fine old cathartic time. And so it was. And, as the thing went up in flames, bystanders came cruising over and started dancing around, and boy, isn't this a great idea and why don't we do it again next year?

Here comes 1988. Two hundred people show up to burn the bejeezus out of what is now a 30-foot effigy officially called "Burning Man." And so it was. Blah, blah, blah.

Same bat time, next bat year. A 40-foot Man is burned as more than 300 seminude beachcombers, many of whom are under the influence of things more potent than fresh ocean air, dance manically. Because Baker Beach technically is part of the

Presidio, the U.S. Military Police show up wanting (for obvious reasons) to know just what the hell is going on here and who is in charge of this chaos. Local TV crews film the MPs' inability to stop 300-plus pagan ritualists from getting jiggy with a 40-foot pyrotechnic graven image. The legend officially goes public.

It's 1990. Again with the 40-foot man. A society of carpenters join the original founder to construct the Man. There are blueprints. An engineer is contracted to build and erect the Man. The Park Police make it clear that they will be goddamned if that burning crap is going to happen again this year—not on *this* beach, it ain't. Some sort of agreement is reached so that they will erect the Man (I'm saying nothing) on the beach, but then will move the Man to the Black Rock Desert in Nevada, one of the nastiest, most godforsaken, most desolate shitholes of a prehistoric lake bed one can imagine. More than 800 people attend the erection of the Man, but only about 90 people make the actual hegira to the desert.

Jump to 1991. Larry Harvey installs the completed statue of the erect Man at Fort Mason in San Francisco. Harvey decides to hell with Baker Beach; he's going straight to the desert again. The Man has been transformed from its original eight-foot woodenness to a towering 40-foot neon behemoth. Due to the expected attendance at the event in the desert, a police force of sorts specifically designed for Burning Man, called the Black Rock Rangers, is founded. The Bureau of Land Management, perplexed as all get out by why in God's name anyone, let alone several thousand anyones, would want to come to this hell pit of dust and grime, requires the organizers to obtain a recreation permit and file an environmental impact report regarding the event. It is at this point that, in the humble opinion of yrs. truly,

Mr. Harvey should have realized things were starting to get out of control, or, rather, very *controlled*. But evidently he did not, 'cuz get ready for 1992.

The Man stays at 40 feet. Additional neon. Additional pyrotechnics. Six hundred folks, with what is assumed to be tons of collective psychological baggage that need a good catharting, trek into the desert to party and walk around naked and burn this big neon thing. The Burning Man "culture" begins to expand, and events include a fashion show (!), an art festival, and now an exploding Man (now *that's* the spirit). The *Black Rock Gazette* is founded. Big goddamn clue that the erection of the Man is getting rather large (as it were). It is around this time that yrs. truly's friends start going to Burning Man and decide it is officially *the* coolest thing in the universe.

And here comes 1993. Now a thousand people are exodusing against all sense to the middle of one of the most inhospitable and blasted areas of the continent. The camp that was previously just an anarchistic jumble now is being laid out and assigned streets. Streets with names. A radio station is established. *Hmmm . . . streets and radio station . . . kinda like the cities these ninnies just came from . . .*

In 1994, a serious organized effort was made by several of my friends to get me to go to Burning Man, which, as we already have established, is purported to be *the* coolest thing in the universe. I decline, citing my appreciation, no, my *need,* for air-conditioning and flushing toilets and such. So, off they go, along with 2,000 other maniacs. A Web site for the Man is started. A documentary is filmed and the event is covered by the international media. Burning, fire dancing, dope, nekkidness, etc., etc.

I don't remember a lot of 1995, but of this I am sure: I once again resisted my friends' pleas to go to the desert and get naked and indulge in illegal substances and dance around a fiery effigy. There was plenty of nakedness and substance use right where I was. Meanwhile, Burning Man becomes "the most populous settlement in Nevada's Pershing County." I have suspicions that the populace of my city block could outnumber the residents of Pershing County in the non–Burning Man seasons, but whatever. The location is dubbed Black Rock City. The *Black Rock Gazette* becomes a daily paper. Various camps develop into "theme camps." Local and federal authorities begin to pay a *lot* of attention to the goings-on in this desert. CNN begins yearly coverage. The Man is ignited with a flamethrower.

Nineteen ninety-six was a big year for the Man. He grew 10 feet and attracted an additional few thousand worshipers. The theme camps are everywhere and people begin performing operas (!). A committee is founded to manage the chaos. Plans are made to relocate the event to the Hualapai Playa to avoid increasing pressure from and tension with law enforcement.

Nineteen ninety-seven is the year of the biggest pressure yet on yrs. truly to go to the desert and get buck-ass nekkid. Though the invitation is tempting, again I resist. My best friend gets the Man tattooed on her leg. Ten thousand people attend the event in the desert, held this time on private land. Attendance is purportedly hurt by the permit process. Despite the "poor" attendance, CNN, ABC's *Nightline*, NBC, *Time* magazine, *The Washington Post*, German TV, and other media from around the world are in attendance and document the whole thing.

On and on it goes into the 21st century, which brings us to the year I get an assignment by a supposedly hip magazine that just found out about Burning Man, their editorial heads apparently having been buried in cultural sand even deeper than the sands of the Black Rock Desert.

Why I didn't want to go and how I lost my pants

I hate to camp. *Goddamn* I hate to camp. I don't mean to asperse or offend those who do, but it just seems like a step in the wrong direction on the evolutionary ladder. It took us millions of years to figure out how to come in out of the rain and the scorching sun and the sleet and the mud and the bugs and the shit, and get our chill on in our air-conditioned havens, toying with our neurochemistry as a hobby and playing video games and eating food that we didn't have to stalk and kill and gut ourselves. I'm proud of human evolution and am in no hurry to go back outside.

Camping, to me, is not getting back to nature . . . it is acting against it.

I don't mean to belabor the point, but I think it's really necessary in order for you to truly understand what a Herculean deal it was for me to decide to go to Burning Man. I really hate the outside. All of it. Every time I walk out of my front door, I say, "Shit." It's true. Ask my friends. I actually stop and say, "Shit." I'm not kidding.

So as you can imagine, kiting off to some savage and blasted moonscape did not have me Rockette-kicking with enthusiasm.

The first thing I discovered was that I had to buy a ticket. This is supposed to be anarchy, and they're selling tickets? Tickets that cost money. Tickets that, when purchased the week before the event, cost $125. That I have to *pay money* to go somewhere that probably sucks puts me in the foulest mood I've been in since the day I found out my proctologist had no depth perception. My friends tried lamely to convince me that going to Burning Man really would be *the* coolest thing in the universe.

"It's beautiful out there," they said.

I sneered. "It's beautiful *here*. It's *hot* there."

"Yeah, but there's really cool art and stuff out there."

"Well, douche, we live in San Francisco . . . rumor has it there's some simply bitching 'art and stuff' here, too."

"You can see nekkid girls walking around."

"Have you been to my apartment lately? I get to see plenty of nekkid girls walking around right here. In fact, for the price of this-here ticket, I could get nekkid girls to do a *lot* more than just walk around."

But I'd said I would go, so I purchased the ticket, coughing up nearly half of my advance from the magazine to do so. Perhaps if they cut back on the amount of printing they did on each ticket, they could bring the cost of admission down a bit. It looks like any other ticket to any other concert or event, except that it is literally *covered* with text, the nature of which makes it more of a death warrant than anything else. And I quote:

**YOU VOLUNTARILY ASSUME THE RISK OF
SERIOUS INJURY OR DEATH BY ATTENDING.**

**You must bring enough food, water, shelter, and first
aid to survive one week in a harsh desert environment.
Commercial vending, firearms, fireworks, rockets, and**

all other explosives are prohibited. Your image may be captured without consent and without compensation. Commercial use of images taken at Burning Man is prohibited without the prior written consent of Burning Man. A Survival Guide will be made available thirty days prior to the event, which you must read before attending. You agree to abide by all the rules in the Survival Guide. This is not a consumer event. Leave nothing behind when you leave this site.

PARTICIPANTS ONLY. NO SPECTATORS.

I looked at the guy who had just sold me this ticket with complete astonishment.

"What the fuck is this?"

He looked back at me without astonishment.

"It's your ticket."

"No, this is a fucking joke. This has got to be a joke."

For the last 10 years, I've been told tall tales about anarchy in the desert, about explosive catharsis, about tear-assing across the playa at speeds higher than your speedometer can register. But there it is, in black and white: no firearms, rockets, or explosives. How in the name of fuck is one supposed to participate in something called Burning Man when one is prohibited from bringing things that burn?

The next day, resigned to my fate, I realized that I had one day to get my logistical shit together. I don't have a car, and I knew I'd need shelter and some way to carry what was sounding like a heap of supplies to the middle of the damn desert. So, I decided to rent a van. That would get me there; I could put all of the gallons of water and packages of jerky I was going to take in the back; and I could take the backseat out and sleep in the sumbitch. Of course, Burning Man occurs on Labor Day weekend, so auto-rental agencies all charge special holiday rates, and it seems several people in the Bay Area had similar ideas, and there was a run on rental vans. I finally found one shady agency that charged $500 for the last van in its lot. The van was the color of a turd that got about two miles to the gallon in the city, and whose horn honked every time I made a right turn. *Joy.*

Next, it's off to the Buy-N-Bulk grocery store, where I purchase five gallons of water and about two pounds of beef jerky (I am *not* buying a stove for this. If I need to cook anything, I'll just lay it on the playa). Couple bags of chips, couple bottles of Pepsi, couple sixers of beer. Toilet paper. Six lighters. Bullets for the gun. Given the way they were ignoring the Not a Consumer Event rule, I figured I could ignore the rest of their bullshit. The Danger Rangers could suck my balls. I'm bringing heat.

The next morning, it is time to go. I wake at 0300h and load the aforementioned supplies, along with some blankets and clothes, into the van, point the thing east, and tear ass toward Nevada.

The rental contract for the van very specifically states: "THIS CAR CAN *NOT* BE DRIVEN OVER STATE LINES." In my heart, I feel that it can. In fact, I know damn good and well that it will just *sail* over the Nevada border. And every time I made a right turn and the horn honked, I felt a little more enthusiastic about doing so. If the honking doesn't stop, I might just drive this fucker right into Utah and leave it floating in the Great Salt Lake.

I managed to beat all of the traffic in San Francisco and Sacramento and Reno. Of course, I had to stop for gas 37 times. But no traffic.

What it's like driving to Burning Man (still written with the intent of eventually getting to the part where I can't find my pants)

First, you drive to Reno. I've done this plenty of times before. A long stretch of boredom through and past Sacramento. And then, the somewhat scenic foothills. There's that buffalo ranch on the right, which is always kind of cool to see. Then, the beautiful Sierras with their winding and circuitous inclines, which, by the way, is pure hell on the ears when you're driving a turd-colored van that honks every time you turn right. Needless to say, the damn thing didn't have a functioning tape deck or CD player, and there is no radio reception in those mountains, so there I was, cringing at the Big Honk every 15 seconds or so. There were more than a few turns when I thought I'd rather endure the fuck-it-all plunge over the side of the cliff than hear that evil god-damned horn one more time. But I persevered.

So, you get to Reno, and you see the pretty lights and the Circus Circus and the advertisements for the All-Your-Fat-Ass-Can-Eat-Steak-and-Eggs-Buffet for $4.99, and boy, do you want to go there instead of the desert. But you've already paid your money, so you keep on going. And, of course, Reno is on the right, and the Pavlovian reaction to the mere thought of the sonic consequences of turning right now are impossible even to consider.

And so you press on past Reno, and things start getting . . . interesting. You go past Sparks, home of the legal brothels (and woefully to the right), and then the desolation begins. For those of us from the überpopulated Bay Area, such desolation can be surprisingly alarming. But that's nothing, because get ready for what's down the road.

Something like 30 miles past Reno, you turn left (amen), and then you drive about 1,000 miles into the middle of shit. The only way to describe things with any hint of accuracy really is "lunar." Every 30 or 40 miles, you see something that you can't really call a "town," but what else are you going to call it? There's a gas station and a few dozen small houses and a small school and a shitload of satellite dishes. There are no pedestrians and the whole thing just *screams* Federal Witness Protection Program.

And then, the towns stop. Another 100 miles and there's an Indian reservation, and *damn!* We're talking generators for all power, fuck knows about air-conditioning, but, of course, one *huge* satellite dish. Dishzilla. Still don't see any actual living people. Haven't since Reno.

Then you start seeing the cows. I've seen a lot of cows while driving around California, but I've never seen cows that literally look *forlorn*. I suspect these are the cows that Sizzler uses. If cows could smoke, these would.

Another 50 miles. Now you start to see cow *carcasses!* Bloated bovine bodies that strayed too far from the water source and just tipped the hell over. And then, after a few more miles, not even carcasses. No birds. No jackrabbits. It's like the plot of a Warhol movie: *nada*.

So, just when you get to the point in the middle of nothing

where you realize that you don't have enough gas to get back to the last gas station, you come across another one of these "towns," this one called Gerlach. And it's actually sizable (relatively, of course). It is the last chance for gas and supplies before Burning Man, which, though only a few miles away, I cannot yet see.

It is worth pausing for a moment to wonder, as I did while pumping yet more gas into the Turd, just how the hell Gerlach subsisted . . . *existed* . . . before Burning Man. During the months of August and September, when BM is being set up, when it occurs, and when it is torn down and cleaned up, Gerlach thrives. But what about the rest of the year? They literally are 100 miles away from *anything*. Again, you can just about choke on the stench of Witness Protection.

So, you gas up in Gerlach, and then it is on to the Big BM site. And it's pretty much what you'd expect. Something like a wrap party for the cast and crew of *The Road Warrior*. I'm in the line of cars to get in for exactly eight seconds before I see my first female nipple. That makes me smile. Not quite worth $125, but I'm trying to be optimistic. But, it is precisely four seconds later that I see my first fully nude male, a hoary bastard whose implicit genitalia are *completely* encanvassed by the apronlike adiposity of his hanging gut. This makes me nauseous and pretty much sets the tone for the rest of the trip.

A Danger Ranger takes my ticket and asks me a couple of questions, like whether or not I have any explosives in my vehicle. And then, get ready for this: She reminds me to please obey the speed limit of five MPH because the traffic stirs up dust.

I begin to growl. Literally. Out loud.

Just a quick recap here: This supposedly mythic and cool

temporary autonomous zone where people come to blow shit up and shoot guns and drive like bastards across the playa and explode things, all with the aim of achieving some sort of massive psychological catharsis, won't let me bring any guns or explosives, and I cannot drive more than five miles per goddamn hour.

I have been here one minute, and I am hot and cranky, and an air of unsubtle menace and piss off exudes from my van.

These feelings only deepen. The friends with whom I will be camping, the crew that has been telling me this is *the* coolest thing in the universe, have told me they will leave a big sign on the area designated for such signs at the entrance of the site telling me where they are camped.

Well.

The message board is about 1,300 square feet of bulletin board covered three layers deep with notes and messages. I guess Day-Glo poster board was not on their list of supplies because there are no "big signs." Not even colored paper. It's been damn near 20 years since I read *The Myth of Sisyphus,* but the theme of it all came back to me very quickly as I spent my first 15 minutes of BM fruitlessly searching for my name scrawled on a piece of paper. Nearby is a girl wearing no shirt. That is supposed to be one of the really cool reasons I am here. But I don't care. Her bare breasts are of such minimal importance right now that, well, that's just a barometer of how lame this already is. There is a perfectly good set of zeppelins in front of me and I don't even care. That is just fundamentally *wrong.* It is then I notice that after a mere 15 minutes, I am getting sunburned. I've gotten plenty of sunburns before—hell, I got sun *poisoning* in Hawaii. But usually the burn and the pain come like an hour after you get out of the sun. Not so here. This desert sun is different. It is *cruel*.

A bit here about naked people in the desert and the merciless sun

The desert sun is a completely different sun than the huge ball of fire around which the rest of the planet rotates. I don't know if it's a difference in the ozone layer here or what, but I am getting seriously fried almost instantaneously. I felt it first on the tops of my feet, at the ankles, where the protection of my shoes ended. Now, a minute later, my shoulders are burned. This sun is a *bitch*. And I am wearing a tank top, shorts, and shoes. There are people walking around completely nude in this prehistoric tanning bed, their reproductive block-and-tackle hanging out like it's made of asbestos. I see numerous naked butts on bicycle seats (all of the seats, by the way, being black leather [!]), cheeks sort of pistoning up and down as the cyclists pedal. I don't believe in karma, per se, but I often have wished that if I were to be reincarnated, I think I would like to come back as the brass pole at my favorite strip club. But if my karmic score comes in on the lower end of the scale, I now fear I may return incarnated as one of these hapless and doomed BM bicycle seats. That is the punishment reserved for the *Ninth* Circle of Hell.

Aside from the deadly sun blast, there is the question of where to put one's keys and water and other belongings when naked. The most common solution here seems to be a backpack, which, in my always-humble opinion, defeats the true purpose and glory of being naked. I mean, if you're going to tote some big-ass backpack around, why stop there? Why not extend the convenience, and throw on some shoes and pants as well? Whether you believe in creation or evolution, you've got to admit Darwin had a pretty irrefutable point when it came to the survival of the fittest. Theoretically, that should mean that the stupid don't survive. But humans, being full of emotion and compassion and mercy and a lot of other tedious baggage, actually seem to *nurture* the stupid *and* allow them to breed. And then you end up like this, with a desert full of naked fat-asses pedaling around and pickling their prostates. I see one guy, fat as Santa, mount a bike and just barely begin to pedal away, when he quickly stands on the pedals, ejecting his corpulent keester from the seat and involuntarily hollering, "Ho! Jesus Christ! Hot potata, hot potata . . . ho . . . Jesus Christ."

I think perhaps one of the most accurate indicators of Darwinian failure in humans is the fetid stench of charred taint at Burning Man. If the term "taint" is unfamiliar to you, take a bike out to the middle of a blazing prehistoric lake bed, let it bake in the sun for an hour or so, nude up, and climb aboard. The part that makes you scream and smell a bit like bacon: that's your taint.

Meanwhile, back at the entrance . . .

The "big sign" my friends left for me to discover (after another grueling 10 minutes under the seemingly magnified sun) is a square of two-ply toilet paper with my name on it with some abstruse descriptions that I can only assume are an address.

I really don't know how I did it, but after driving around for about an hour, I managed to find them. I pulled up to the camp in the big greenish-brown Turd and they all came running out of their shaded shelters like the crew of *Gilligan's Island* to a Coast Guard chopper that just landed on the beach. They all are covered in dust. I don't think they are particularly overjoyed to see *me*: They all had been here for a week already, and I suspect had grown bored and were on the verge of lunging at one another the way people get after they are around one another for too long. That or they took my horn honk when I made a right turn into the camp as a form of greeting. Nothing could have been further from the truth. I want to kick each one of them in the pants (would that they were wearing pants), and I would, but it's too goddamn hot. I grunt at them and head for the back of the Turd and open a beer. I may as well have doused myself with gasoline and pulled out a lighter.

"No, dude! You don't wanna drink *beer!* You wanna drink water. Just drink lots of water."

About eight people say this to me at the same time. It is obvious that they are suffering from paranoid delusions and sunstroke psychosis. These are the same people who have helped me inhale, snort, and swallow some of the most insidious and dangerous recreational chemicals ever invented, in quantities that would have made Timothy Leary balk. I am officially disgusted. No guns, no explosives, no driving fast, and now these weenies won't even let me drink a beer.

It is 11:30 a.m., and it is 112 degrees Fahrenheit, and I have just driven seven hours in a Turd with a horn that honked every time I turned right, and I have sunburned feet, and I have to drive five (five!) miles per hour, and *fuck you*. Give me my bottle opener.

They shake their collective heads as if I'm preparing to put out an electrical fire by pissing on it.

In light of their protests, rather than the one beer I had planned, I throw four beers back in quick and defiant seriatim. Nothing happens. I don't collapse from dehydration. I don't burst into flames. I don't die. I don't even get buzzed. I throw the empties over my shoulder, rip the seats out of the van and set up a lean-to shade shelter over the seats, sit down, and ask, after a Wagnerian belch, "Why is this fun?"

The question hangs there in that stagnant desert air like a big shit piñata, with no one daring to take a swing at the thing. My companions are nonplussed. Evidently, I don't get the obvious. Perhaps it is just too hot to talk. Which is, more or less, the case. I open another beer.

It is then that the first of what will be many dust- and windstorms occurs. It is truly impressive, if for no other reason than you can *see* it coming: this Old Testament wall of dust and doom headed inevitably directly *at you*. A kind-of verbal Emergency Broadcast Warning spreads quickly across the entirety of the BM. My friends head for their tents and I climb into the Turd. It is amazing. The dust is so fine that it gets *into* the Turd somehow, despite all of the doors and windows being closed. It is almost like a gas. A minute later, the storm is over. People emerge from their hovels. Everything that wasn't covered in dust before now is. You can *taste* it. My shade shelter now is somewhere in Montana, and as the fog of dust is clearing, the sun begins burning things again.

There I sit, pissed. Occasionally, companions wander over and ask after my well-being and mood. I glare and threaten to pounce. They ask me if there is anything they can do. My only response is, of course: "Drugs."

As the sun goes down, things begin to liven up. It seems

that at the Big BM, the strategy is to sit around moribundly all day, moving as little as possible and being flat, as mammals are wont to do when the temperature gets to be as hot as a Benihana griddle. Then, when the sun goes down, and the cool desert breeze kicks in, the party begins.

What Burning Man is like at night

Imagine if a squadron of jets napalmed the Las Vegas strip and you've pretty much got it. The only sources of light out there are fire and that provided by generators. And the sort of light that comes from people who are willing to pay for and cart out numerous and huge generators into the middle of the desert ain't reading light. There are fully functioning nightclubs out here, complete with elaborate state-o'-the-art sound systems and IntellaBeam lasers. There are disco balls. It is insane, and beautiful. But yet again it contributes to my general problem with this whole thing: All of these nightclubs and such are in the city where we just came from . . . except back there you can drink a cocktail without having to worry about scooping a layer of dust off the surface before every sip, and the whole works doesn't shut down every half hour for fear of being blown into the next state by a windstorm.

And for the same money some of these people invest in generators and sundry other equipment (and we are talking in the tens-of-thousands-of-dollars range for some people), they could do so much more so much more easily in a place that already *has* power and flushing toilets (which, by the way, is going to have to be dealt with sooner or later here, so I'll do it later, in a section clearly marked for the Big BM's toilet situation, so consider yourself warned and brace yourself).

Burning Man's existential hypocrisy aside for a moment, the place *is* pretty groovy at night.

As my friends and I ambulate around, we see fire jugglers, fire eaters, and one guy who sets light to his penis and whose (I'm just guessing here) girlfriends eat the fire, fellating his fleshy torch, thus bringing the added performance-art aspect of sword swallowing into the picture.

For the first time in 24 hours, I'm beginning to think that this wasn't the biggest waste of $700-plus ever.

We come across (not literally) an animated effigy of former president Bill Clinton that, when you shake its hand, squirts a jizzlike substance from a phallus that pops with surprising speed out of his pants.

More peripatetic wandering. I am staying very close to my friends because everything looks pretty much the same and there are no landmarks and it is as dark as a well-digger's ass on a moonless night and there is simply no way I will ever find our camp again without them.

It is then that we happen upon a seminar instructing campers on how to properly make and throw a Molotov cocktail. *NOW we're talking!* I am the son of an Irish Protestant father and an Irish Catholic mother, so the knowledge of appropriate ratios of gasoline to thickening agent in such a combustible concoction is almost innate with me. But what makes this fun is the target, which target changes nightly. Tonight, the target is a wooden mock-up of Ronald McDonald, grinning like a psychotically manic Buddha, one hand holding a Happy Meal, the other hand giving the Finger. This is a BYOB seminar, so people are showing up with everything from beer bottles to those huge jugs of Livingston Cellar's hooch. One dolt brings a box of wine: the kind with the spigot on the side. No, that won't do, he is told, but is congratulated on his spirit. I suggest that he replace Ronald as the target, but those who hear my idea just glare disdainfully. Apparently this is politically correct terrorism. What else would you expect from such a group? Tattoos and piercings and insurrectionist trappings aside, we're just talking about the next generation of hippies. *Anarchy! But don't break any of our laws. No cash exchanges allowed at Burning Man! But cough up $100-plus to get in. Let's blow things up! But don't bring any explosives or guns . . . that would break the carefully established laws of our anarchy. Make Molotov cocktails! But don't ever even joke about actually using them against anything.*

I loathe this kind of shit. What am I doing here? *Who are these dilettantes?* And that's when it hits me like a wall. I know who they are. And I know what this is. Burning Man is where all of those virginal nerds from those insipid Renaissance Pleasure Faires of the world go during the off-season. These are the people who carry swords around as costume pieces, but get frightened when I pull out a functioning switchblade. These are the people who will (and this actually happened with a former roommate) challenge you to a "sword fight" with bamboo practice swords and then cry foul (or sometimes just cry) when you clock them on the side of the head. "You're not supposed to really *hit* people!" And here they are, cheering at people throwing explosives at a wooden clown and thinking they're anarchist prophets and carrying knives on their belts and looking forward to a huge explosion and five-story fire, but they've got to leave the day after the burn to get back to San Francisco to protest some war or other. Overgrown adolescents who never learned that toys are for playing and weapons are for killing and

Molotov cocktails are not used as entertainment in the real world . . . not in real anarchy. They bemoan the image of "the ugly American," but what more egregious display of ignorant self-gratifying indulgence is there than throwing Molotov cocktails for "fun." These are history's misfits, and I pretty much hate them.

But not nearly as much as they hate Ronald McDonald. They want Ronald *dead*, but not until he has suffered. I talk briefly to the teacher of this seminar, who tells me that tomorrow night's target is the Pope; and the following night is Bill Buckner.

More ambulation. There are several raves going on. All in all, it is fine. A bit like the midway at the state fair if you were on acid—which, by the way, my cohorts, who had vehemently poo-pooed my consumption of beer, had failed miserably to procure. No drugs whatsoever. Truth is, I don't think they've even tried.

Eventually we wander back to our camp, and I climb in the Turd and go to sleep, quickly and soundly. I sleep like the dead. Like a baby. Like a dead baby. Surrounded by hippies.

Day two and the arrival of James the Mushroom Man

Everyone wakes at almost the exact same time in the desert because of the sudden increase in temperature when the sun comes over the horizon. Then, everyone waddles over to the shade to drink water and bitch and paint themselves with henna, or eat cocktail weenies or whatever until the sun goes back down so they can party some more. I use the time to write various things, including a death threat to the editor who sent me out here and a letter to Kristoffer, the theme of which is that the cool stuff I've seen here has been worth about 17 bucks and I wish to Christ I had the other 600 or so back so I could go on a cruise to Mexico or some real vacation.

It is then that I notice there are no insects at Burning Man. Not one. Yesterday, I tied a trash bag to the antenna of the Honking Turd, and it quickly filled with banana peels and jerky wrappers and beer bottles and whatnot. A windstorm that hit the camp during the night ripped the bag from the antenna, leaving it lying open on the playa floor. I am simply in too foul a mood to put it back up, so there it stays . . . for three days. And it is *untouched.* No animals. No raccoons. No ants. Even insects are too intelligent to go to that goddamn place.

As I'm writing this down, I hear my name spoken in a nearby shade structure. I look up to see my associates pointing me out to a lugubrious-looking fellow with a shaved head and sunken eyes. He doesn't look like law enforcement, so I don't run. He walks over to me and introduces himself with a thick English accent: "Jayson? My name is James. I was told you might be interested in buying some mushrooms."

I've never really dealt with mushrooms before, so I don't know how much to buy or how much to pay. But James is very congenial and avuncular and under the influence of his own product, and for $40 gives me a pretty sizable bag of psychedelic fungus.

"How much of this do I take?" I ask James.

"Well," he says as he opens the bag and begins separating bits and pieces and stems and whatnot. "I would take this much to start, and then I just usually nibble as needed."

Well, that sounds like fine advice to me, Jamie, my friend.
James shakes my hand and departs, and my friends look at me
with mixtures of surprise and dark expectation. *Fuck those tee-*
totaling freaks . . . I'm sick of beef jerky anyway . . . today, I shall
have mushrooms for breakfast.

As I start gagging these horrid things down, I can hear
numerous expressions literally and thematically of "Aw shit"
and "Here we go." Never mind "nibbling as needed," I eat the
whole gruesome package. A quick note to those of you who
have never eaten magic mushrooms: They taste *exactly* like
what they are, which is fungus that grew from cowshit in a pas-
ture in Seattle.

Today is far cooler, meteorologically, at least, than yesterday,
and so our camp decides to take a walk. Enough drug-trip stories have been written about the Nevada desert, and you can
probably imagine the sorts of neurological perception-is-reality
craziness that went on in and around my fragile psyche, so in
the interest of brevity, I'll just give you some bulleted highlights:

- After a solid hour of bansheelike cackling, I swear to
  Christ that I can see the ocean. I know we are in the middle of the desert and there isn't even a puddle for about
  1,000 miles, but dammit, there it is. And not only can I
  see the ocean, but over there is an entire New England
  seaport town. Looks like Gloucester, MA. My friends are
  very understanding and cool as I tell them this.

- It occurs to me that we are all now living inside Salvador
  Dalí's greatest painting and have been all of our lives. In all
  probability, Mr. Dalí is still very much with us on another

plane and we are just figures in a painting that is being stared at and studied and appreciated by stern-looking art fans in a museum in another time.

- It occurs to me that I've always wanted to eat human flesh. Just once. But I always disappoint myself by chickening out at the last minute whenever the opportunity presents itself.

- This group is far too slow for me and I need to be alone, so I bolt from the group and tear ass straight into the desert because it has just occurred to me that I am Jesus and I need to talk to Dad.

- Somehow I end up in a complete stranger's tent with no pants.

This last one is rather key. I have no idea how I got into this person's tent, and I have no idea at what point or even how I lost my pants, but I suddenly was quite grateful for the "no firearms" rule at the Big BM and for the Christlike kindness and patience of the guy who found a total stranger high as a kite with no pants sitting in his tent wrapping himself with toilet paper.

I guess my plan had been to simply wear the toilet paper in lieu of pants (the funny thing is that no one out here would have even looked twice), but this guy was kind enough to give me a pair of shorts, on the condition that I give him his evidently much-needed toilet paper back. "And no . . . don't worry about trying to roll it back up."

Somehow, I find my way back to my campsite and am discomfited that absolutely no mission had been launched to determine my whereabouts.

"We knew you'd get back eventually. Besides, you said that if anyone tried to follow you, you would eat them on a kabob."

It had a ring of truth to it, so I just climbed into the Turd and slept, and waited for nightfall.

The day of the Burn

As grumpy and disappointed as I've been up until this point, I'm trying my hardest to keep an open mind. After all, this is $700 worth of fun I'm supposed to be having, dammit, and if there is any possibility of having it, I will do so.

Day three begins and progresses as usual. Everyone wakes with the sudden heat. People trudge with the slothlike movement of people who only move when they must and that typically is to go to the bathroom. Ah, the bathroom. We may as well get on with it.

What it's like to micturate or otherwise evacuate at Burning Man

Unfortunate, at best. Horrible, at normal. Miasmic. Here's the deal: Throughout the vast site of the Big BM, there are obtrusive rows of light blue Porto-Sani-Flush outhouses, many of which are used to define the edges of the established "streets" or perimeters of blocks that have been set up by the organizers of the "anarchy." They are state-of-the-art (for lack of a better term) in the science of human-waste receptacles, and are as efficient and ventilated as imaginable while still providing a modicum of privacy. And I'm sure they are not half bad during the first few days of the week of Burning Man, when they arrive completely decontaminated and remain relatively so, simply because of the lesser number of people that are actually in attendance and pooping during the early stages of the event. But then Labor Day weekend arrives, along with an additional 20,000 or so partygoers with their anxious anuses, and things can get mighty nasty around the Porto-Sani-Flush boxes. *Mighty* nasty. By the day I arrive, things have gotten so bad that there is a noticeable dearth of campsites in what would otherwise be coveted real estate downwind of the temporary sanitation facilities.

They set up these phalanxes of flatulence and voidance at the beginning, and just let 'em fill up until the end of the event, when they come in with huge cranes and flat-bed trucks, and take these things some . . . place, which place, if it wasn't awful before, is most certainly henceforth the most-assiest place on the planet.

A lot of what going to Burning Man seems to be about is being or at least looking cool. I have found that there is no possible way to project even the slightest hint of coolness whilst trudging toward the dreaded wall of Blue Doom, carrying a roll of toilet paper. This is tantamount to walking into some concert dressed entirely in black with a shirt that (in white lettering) says, "I have to poop." I don't know—maybe this is saying more about *me* than anything else, but it makes sense. All of the work done by dressing up in cool Middle-Eastern clothing or being covered with rugged and weathered black leather Road Warrior armor is instantly undone by picking up a totem of screaming white toilet paper (the desert, like the sea, is almost exclusively composed of one color, making all other colors inordinately accentuated and shocking) and taking the "I gotta take a dump" hike.

But this brings up something even more gruesome. There you are, standing in the inevitable line at the poopers, making no eye contact with your fellow linemates, each one clutching his or her own roll of toilet paper, waiting with equal amounts of hopeful or impatient expectation and inevitable dread for the next blue door to creak open invitingly. Something you learn very quickly in this line is that what comes out of the most recently opened door matters a great deal. The best one can hope for is that some reasonably well-dressed (and at the Big BM, this could mean a variety of things) and small personage will emerge quickly and daintily from the darkness of the crap closet. That's the best-case scenario. Then, there's the worst-case scenario, which happened to me not once, but *three* times in my jaunts to the outhouses. Just try to imagine this . . .

There you are, standing lamely in the line of lientery, baking in the scorching desert sun, knowing that the horrid contents of the Porto-Sani-Flush are baking in even more dreadful ways. And, you're standing there pathetically holding a roll of toilet paper. And, you're next in line. Plosive expulsions and almost immediate splats can be heard, but not pinpointed to any specific door. And, the door to the next-available stink closet opens. And, out lumbers this huge naked hairy beast of a man, apron of fat hanging and flapping over his groin. He emits a circumstantially disgusting exhale of contentment that only serves to punctuate what happens next: He has ridden a bike from a distant camp, and now remounts the bicycle and his horrid overhanging glutes piston away.

If you dare turn around and look at your fellow line-inhabitants, you will see their forlorn eyes brighten ever-so-slightly into an unmistakable "better-you-than-me" look. But, looking at other people in this line is as big a faux pas as making eye contact with people in adult bookstores.

So there you are, having to enter what is sure to be a miasma of prostatic secretion.

It is not uncommon to see people take a visibly noticeable huge breath before entering the Porto-Sani-Flush. Some even pull the collars of their shirts (assuming they are wearing shirts) up over their mouths and noses, just in case their agendas in the outhouses take longer than their lung capacities provide for.

There are myriad other problems and horrors involved in the egestive rituals at the Big BM, but I probably have already gone into too much detail, which detail hopefully will be edited out by my tasteful and persuasive editor. Suffice it to say, yrs. truly held out for as long as possible, and when as long as possible arrived, he inconspicuously placed a roll of two-ply into a backpack with a bottle of water and headed (rather quickly) into the unseeable regions of the desert and communed with nature. Yes, I am guilty . . . I left a trace. But my conscience is quite clear and I sleep very well at night.

Anyway, getting back to the actual burning of the BM

So the sun goes down, and there is a palpable increase in the energy and aura and electricity of the populace. The psychogenesis of this partially (and obviously) is because the five-story effigy that has been towering over us and been the center of all activity, and that essentially is the reason everyone is here is going to be cathartically dispatched in a fiery burst of ignited gas and exploding neon. The other reason that people are so excited (and many will deny this, but I know that it is at least partially true because I was told so by hippies with BM tattoos themselves) is that this hell which people paid to get into, and which is supposed to be way more fun than Disneyland, is, thank Christ, about to end, and we have lasted it out and now we can get the hell back to civilization and running water and toilets and climate control and beds with springs and people will be clothed unless we really, really want them not to be.

At twilight, people wander over to the Man, either individually or as camps. There are lots of poles, crosses (life-sized, on occasion), torches, and all species of glow sticks. This is the night they pull out all of the stops. And at a place that exists, at least theoretically, to pull out all of the proverbial stops, well, it can be quite a sight.

Many of the people in my camp are fire dancers, which, on the one hand, seems kind of cool, I guess. It looks cool at night in the desert and that's what counts, I suppose. So here we go, swinging fire (yrs. truly is handed some sort of bamboo pole with a peculiarly colored peach glow stick tied to the top). The result is that I join in the stroll toward the Man carrying what looks like a radioactive hot dog on a disproportionately large stick. About one-quarter of the way to the Man, I realize that I look like even more of a knob than usual carrying the neon weenie on a steeek, so I ditch it in a random camp.

Eventually we make it to the Man, where a few thousand people have already gathered. A perimeter has been set up around the Man to keep people at a "safe" distance from the powerful pyrotechnic heroics that are about to occur. My group finds a relatively unpopulated spot, sets up its own subtle

perimeter, and begins fire dancing. All is cool except for two
things:

1. They are not quite experienced enough to have this art
   down to a science. More precisely, when they dip their
   torches and other fire-swinging devices into their fuel can-
   isters, they fail to shake off enough excess fuel. The result
   is that once these things are set ablaze and start a-
   swingin', several spectators, including yrs. truly, get hit
   with supernumerary droplets of flame, which, if you've
   ever made bacon (or anything else involving grease and a
   griddle) whilst nude, you can begin to understand. Except
   it is much worse.
2. Several people are in states so altered they barely can form
   sentences. There are two reasons for this:
   a. Tonight is the big blowout; and
   b. You've got to do all of the drugs you haven't already
      done tonight, because Nevada's Finest are out in force
      and pretty much waiting for anything that looks like
      erratic driving. But anyway . . .

So, these people are just *wasted* and have decided that fire is
their new and very beautiful friend. They want to touch it, and
so they try. They try to catch passing torches of flame. "It's
beauooooootiful!" remarks one drug casualty as he takes a
flaming torch in his palm. I take dark comfort in knowing he
will come to in the morning, after a sleepless and intensely
introspective night, and realize he is two hours away from the
nearest real hospital with the skin of his left hand scorched to
brutal boils and blisters.

And so, finally, the electricity in the air increases and it becomes evident that if the management doesn't torch this big neon bastard, the unwashed and dusty shall rise up and torch it for them. Several smaller explosions occur as a kind of opening act, but this crowd, many of whom have been enduring intolerable desert conditions for a week or more, are in no mood for any opening acts. The time has come to burn the BM.

A man (real) appears between the Man's (Big BM's) legs and does some sort of manic interpretive dance. It is clear that he either is made entirely of marshmallows or is wearing a really puffy asbestos suit (from my angle, he looks like the Michelin Man during amphetamine psychosis). He's running around between the Man's legs with a couple of torches. He then, amazingly, sets *himself* ablaze (the asbestos suit being pushed to the limit having been covered in gasoline or some similar accelerant) and instantaneously becomes a walking ball of fire.

First, he sort of walks/stumbles (as one who is consumed in flames [asbestos protection be damned] tends to do). He touches the Man's leg, and it catches fire. The crowd literally roars. I've never heard a crowd actually, literally, roar until this, and it is surreal and awesome.

Then he stumbles/staggers (screw the asbestos suit . . . he's *got* to be feeling this heat) to the other leg. It takes quite a while for that leg to catch on fire: Just long enough for me to think that someone is going to rush up with a fire extinguisher and put him (the man, not the Man) out, when the leg finally catches fire and the whole Man just fucking *explodes!* I am never able to confirm what happened to the flaming Michelin Man, but as far as I'm concerned, he is presumed dead.

So the Man is a-burnin', and everyone is cheering like Jesus and Elvis just showed up with big secrets to tell. And BM pessimist that I am, a five-story effigy engulfed in flames, with pyrotechnics shooting out of what I would consider painful orifices out of which to have pyrotechnics shoot, is quite a sight to behold. But then all hell breaks loose.

Within minutes, enough of the Man has burned so that its skeletal infrastructure collapses. The Man falls forward at the waist in a way that was clearly unplanned. Everyone (except for me) surges forward, the illusion of a safety perimeter being demolished. Which is fine, except let's not forget that this thing has been packed with various fireworks and rockets which now, instead of shooting gloriously toward the heavens as intended, are shooting directly *into* the crowd. This strikes me as darkly hilarious as I walk in some direction, *any* direction away from this madness. I don't know it then, but I will not see any members of my camp for at least a week, hundreds of miles from here.

I wander around looking for the nearest free-hippie-love-fest I had been told the playa is just frothing with on the night of the Burn. The closest I come (cue rimshot here) is a rave camp with a girl who looks just like Star from *The Lost Boys* movie who is dancing topless and well, and we are giving each other the Eyes. But, it turns out, that is all we will be giving each other once her boyfriend/whatever shows up and starts dancing with her and just ruins everything.

I keep wandering around to various camps, including something called "Bianca's Love Shack," which has signage that promises sex to all who enter. It does not, however, detail just what *kind* of sex, and I find myself in what amounts to an opium den filled with a bunch of guys who appear almost as desperate and pathetic as I am.

I see one or two other cool things, but nothing even worth mentioning, and somehow I make my way back to the Honking Turd and say fuck it and go to sleep. I am disappointed.

I wake before anyone else in my camp (none of whom got to sleep until many hours after I did) and pack up the Turd and tear-ass back to San Francisco, passing on the left, one hand on the horn, the other out the window, middle finger extended.

Kiss my pucker, Fizzle Man

There is something (in fact a great deal) to be said about the psychological release gained by going to a sparsely or unpopulated place and doing things you couldn't or wouldn't normally do (e.g., chucking Molotov cocktails at papal effigies or walking around in a suit made of bubble wrap). But when it becomes an *event,* and that event becomes so popular that its own attendance is greater than the population of the city you just came from, it ends up being an environment just as and, in the case of the Big BM, even *more* restrictive than what you are claiming to be escaping. Whatever spiritual and psychological substance it may have had in the past now is long lost, leaving nothing but yet another nudist gathering minus climate control and plumbing. Burning Man is to anarchy and total artistic expression what Blink 182 is to punk rock: a joke ignored by all who have experienced the Real Thing.

All things considered, the Big BM has been a truly lame fuck-around that set me back $700, which I am not really expecting ever to see again. And rather than some groovy love-feeling for my fellow freaks, I hate the outside more than ever. I still stop and say "Shit" every time I walk out the front door. I'm not kidding . . . check it out.

Here is an actual transcript of what happened this afternoon when I left the house for the first time today:

Me: Shit

Stripper [somewhat urgently, as if expecting that I locked my keys in the house]: What?

Me: It's still here.

Stripper: What is?

Me [waving vaguely]: Everything.

Stripper: What do you mean, "everything"?

Me [waving hands more aggressively and contemptuously at the world]: The outside.

A Spy in the House of Love

"You *still* haven't paid me for that nudist nightmare in Nevada yet!"

"Give us a couple of weeks. You'll get your money."

"And that's when I'll do another story for you. In the meantime, you can kiss my squirrel."

"But we *need* this story for the next issue, the 'Spring Fever' issue. Our investors are going to be making their decision about the funding based on what they see. And, they want to see naked girls and stories about sex. With girls. Sex with naked girls."

"No way. Forget it."

"But, you don't even know what the assignment is yet."

"Are you deaf? It doesn't matter what the assignment is. My rent is due, you pimp!"

"Listen, Jayson, I'm *begging* you. Please. We *need* this."

"*We* don't need shit. *I* need my money, and *you* need a kick in the ass with a really pointy shoe."

"That's fair. That's fair. I deserve that. You're right. You are absolutely right. We'll just figure something out . . ."

"Your guilt means nothing to me. I have no capacity for guilt. I am without conscience. But that is not your concern. What is of your concern is that I am also very much without any money."

"Have you ever thought perhaps one might have to do with the other: no guilt, no money?"

"What the hell does that mean?"

"Never mind. Too much pot. Listen . . . three hundred dollars. Up front. Cash. Today."

"No. Forget it. Save your fetid breath. I am not going anywhere until I get paid for that insipid Nevada nightmare. That was supposed to be my summer vacation, you know? I'm not going anywhere anymore for you."

I hear the click of a lighter and the deep draw of breath as if through a pipe. He then speaks in that weird strained stoner tone without exhaling:

"Not even to a sex club?"

"No, not even to . . . a . . . did you say sex club?"

He exhales hugely.

"Bet your ass. An *amazing* sex club."

"Horseshit. Sex clubs are shams. Money-making shams."

"Not this one. This one is the real deal. At least, that's what everybody says. Only you can judge. That's why *you* have to go."

"*Four* hundred dollars. Cash. Today. Right now."

"Done. Two thousand words."

"I hate you."

"Come get your money, go to the club, spend the night, do what you do, and pound out a story by Monday."

"What the hell does *that* mean . . . 'do what you do'? What exactly do I do?"

"Are you saying you don't know what you're doing?"

"Eat a bag of fuck, you pathetic hesher."

"See you soon. Hurry up; one of our advertisers paid for

this month's space with a 10-foot bong, and I want to try it out. I need someone to light it."

I was screwed yet again. Forced into literary prostitution for survival by Reality and an unscrupulous editorial pimp whose largest piece of office equipment was now a water pipe. Fine. I'll go to this club. The Antichrist knew I had no choice. It was either sit in my apartment in brutal sobriety, alone, listening to the landlord gnaw on the doorknob, or go pick up a bunch of cash, light the bong from hell, and go to a sex club. What would you do?

What I know about the Edgewater West Adult Resort before I get there

It is a clothing-optional swingers' resort where couples parade around in various stages of undress, and look both at and for other couples in similar states of undress with whom to have sex. What makes this place different from other "adult resorts," and the thing that allows me to show up alone, is that the Edgewater is not exclusively for couples. Single people are welcome to look for love as well. That typically spells bad news at any sort of "adult"-oriented event. Usually such events are promoted by flyers featuring one or more leather- and lingerie-clad, impeccably proportioned females in erotic poses holding weapons or marital aids or esoteric devices that could fall into either category. One is led to believe that not only will these particular ladies be there, but they will bring all of their equally stunning friends, and seeing this flyer will encourage other, similar women to show up, looking for a good time. And men, being simple enough to actually think that any woman who sees this flyer would actually go to such an event without either boyfriend or pay or both, would also think, "Oooh lookie here . . . this looks like a good time," and call all of their friends and they all show up expecting some nonexistent smorgasbord of sex. Of course, the event that promised a paradise on par with what suicide bombers are told shall be their reward in the afterlife ends up being nothing more than an army of hoary voyeurs with protruding guts, fat hands and disposable cameras, clicking off snapshots and masturbating like chimpanzees. Packs of swarthy men whose only English seems to be "How much" prowl the grounds each night, in their tragicomic quests for love. I was not eager to join these sorry ranks, but an assignment is an assignment. Besides, having seemingly exhausted all traditional routes to a meaningful relationship, I figured: what the hell.

I had been told that there are two important rules at the Edgewater:

1. Respect the Code of the Windows: If the curtains are closed, fuck off. If the curtains are open, you are invited to look in and see what's going on. If there's something going on, feel free to stay and watch. If both the curtains and sliding glass door are open, well . . . come on in and say hello.
2. Stay out of the hot tub.

1936h—Register at the front desk and prepare for love

Checking into the Edgewater West is uneventful. In fact, as I was signing the register, I wondered if perhaps unwary travelers, tired from a long day's drive, might somehow accidentally find themselves at this desk, wife and kids still back in the car, signing up for what they are hoping will be a long night's rest, woefully ignorant of the bacchanalian rumpus occurring just on the other side of the gate.

I am given a key to Room 136, and I drive around to the back of the hotel. The resort is laid out essentially like a baseball diamond, with the rooms comprising the area between first and third base, a pool and hot tub at shortstop, and the main building that houses the office and nightclub composing an egregiously disproportionate home plate. My room is halfway between first and second, on the ground floor. I am let into the "Guests Only" parking lot by a kid who might look 18 if he didn't shave for a week and smoked three packs a day. He eyes me suspiciously. Behind him, in the distance, I see a small gathering of naked people in and around what I'm guessing is the hot tub.

To be honest, I expected much worse out of an adult motel. I imagined roaches, water damage, and a vibrating bed that accepts quarters and doesn't so much massage as simulate the Great Quake of 1906. The Edgewater has none of those things, but it is not without its adolescent love gimmicks. The most noticeable difference between Room 136 and your average Best Western room is the presence of two very large mirrors placed on the walls around the bed. The mirrors are placed at conspicuously low levels, so that it is simply impossible to use them for any "conventional" purpose, like checking out how one's outfit looks or primping one's coif. Which brings us uncomfortably to the next stop on our little tour: I'm not sure what the sheets are made of, but I think it is some form of plastic. Not that they're dirty: They just somehow lend themselves more to some sort of scientific examination or crime-scene usage than they do to sleep.

The TV in Room 136 officially gets several channels, but the only one that comes in with any sort of clarity is the 24-hour hard-core-porn channel, which suits me just fine. If the going gets too strange out there by the hot tub as the night wears on, I know I can always abscond back here, crawl under the plastic sheets, and rest quietly in the soft light of the pornocopia on Channel 3.

2007h—What to wear; what to wear?

A word about clothing-optional places in general. I have been to a number of such gatherings: resorts, beaches, Burning Man, whatever. The majority of the people walking around nekkid are the ones you most wish had opted for clothes. Besides that, I like pockets. The whole point of nekkidness is to feel unencumbered, is it not? How unencumbered can you feel, lugging around your wallet and your keys and your lucky rubber and your switchblade? How do you hold your beer? I'd feel pretty fucking cumbered without pockets. Besides, it is always better to conceal than to reveal, and I'm here to get lucky. So I opt to wear my usual club gear: lots of black. Lots of pockets.

2013h—Peripateticism

Taking a stroll around the grounds, so far I see mostly couples. Apparently, most of the singles don't show up until the cabaret show, which show is scheduled to start in about 45 minutes (this also might have something to do with the rates: the rooms here are about $100 a night, whereas the show tickets are a mere $40). As I walk around and look at the expressions on these couples' faces, I feel like Spock whenever he and Kirk would beam down to some idyllic utopia whose populace knew nothing but love. The people here seem just a little too happy. I think it's the way they look at me extendedly and say "hi" in the same tone one usually would reserve for ordering a decadent ice-cream dessert.

2019h—Mischievous

A dancer who works at the club introduces herself as "Mischief." She has erumpent breasts, and her perfume smells like a three-day weekend. I introduce myself as a writer on assignment, and she offers to give me a tour and I drool in acceptance. She is barefoot and walks on her tiptoes. I have been here for less than an hour and already have found true love.

The tour is brief since the grounds are fairly small. Highlights include a koi pond noticeably lacking in koi, and a pool that is being "worked on" and is noticeably lacking in water, and a hot tub that I can't really see because there is such a large crowd around it. But I hear extreme bubbling and frothing. Mischief leads me away quickly.

2100h—Showtime

Each week the Edgewater features adult cabaret entertainment in its sizable nightclub. There usually is the $40 cover charge, but Mischief has brought me in as a guest, through a back entrance, and I take this as a declaration of love. She is emceeing this week's show, which begins with two first-time strippers who are 18 and 19, respectively. They are followed shortly by two other dancers who are slightly older and much more experienced. Then comes the featured dancer, an up-and-coming porn-starlet named Summer Collins. There is something about Summer that is really bothering me, and it is not until I get a lap dance from her later that I figure it out: She has the smile, personality, overall look, and voice of Cindy Brady. Not that that is a bad thing. In fact, getting a lap dance from Cindy Brady after she has had D-cup implants bolted onto her chest is a fantasy I didn't even know I had, but I guess it was there all the time. Though, a little goes a long way. She seems to think that Mischief and I are "together," and wants us to "hang out" with her and her boyfriend later. Mischief just smiles and shrugs maybe.

2203h—Baiting the hooker, er, baiting the hook

The show is over, and Mischief and I are doing what she calls "trolling." This involves simply slowly ambling around the grounds, looking into people's open windows, and exchanging meaningful glances with other singles and couples. She explains to me that the single guys here are somewhat of an annoyance to the couples that frequent the place, because the single guys are pretty much all of the aforementioned masturbating voyeur species. But, because I appear to be part of a couple, members of other couples don't feel threatened and seem to be interested. However, I find there is another reason we are getting so many looks. A lot of these people come here *every* *weekend*. So it is an intimate little community. They know one another. And they can spot "virgins" (first-timers) right away. And first-timers are considered to be a bit of a sexual delicacy because (get this) they are presumed "clean" (disease-free) and can therefore be "ridden bareback" (no condom). I grimace at this, and Mischief is quick to tell me that most of what she sees and hears about and participates in is very safe and responsible and so on, but still . . .

2221h—*Margarita*

We come to a room with about a dozen people in it, all either just this side of unconsciousness or afflicted with a wicked logorrhea that makes one suspect strong stimulant snorting. The occupants, who all recognize Mischief and invite us in, are evenly divided between male and female, with the ethnic division including both Caucasian and Hispanic. The man in whose name the room is registered is one of the roundest people I have ever seen. Literally round. Imagine a big circle with another smaller circle on top of it. He is a very cool Mexican guy named Jorge who subtly rules the room in a manner similar to Jabba the Hutt. I never see him anywhere except in his chair, amorphous arms folded on his substantial gut, smiling (Jorge, not his gut). His "significant other" is another "substantial" person, an attractive Hispanic female named Gina. An associate of theirs named Pablo is on the other side of the room, and though his exact relationship is never made clear, his bearing is that of a bodyguard. But that is not what matters now. What matters now is a blow-up doll and a stolen tank of helium. But we'll get to that in a minute.

I am given a beer.

"You wanna line?" asks Jorge.

"Sure," I say, not wanting to be rude. A line of what I don't know, but somehow I think that to ask would make me seem like an asshole. Never look a gift rail in the mouth.

Jorge gives a nod, and Pablo hands Mischief a small plastic bag. Mischief is bent over a table, cutting lines on a Massive Attack CD case. Her breasts shake as she chops, and I fail miserably at not staring. I always have had a soft spot for large-breasted women chopping narcotics. Turns out she has a serious talent for this. She slides the CD case across the table to me, passing a gold straw along with it. I cannot tell what the fine white powder is—coke, speed, or heroin. I'm guessing coke.

Wrong.

Speed.

Ouch.

It's going to be a long night.

After Mischief hoovers another one, she slides the CD case back across the table to me.

"Here," she says, "do another one."

A really long night.

And now to the business at hand, which is not what you— or at least I—would expect at a swingers' club.

This whole weird group is trying to get as much helium as possible into a life-sized, anatomically horrific love doll.

Apparently there is some conflict with the people upstairs, and they are going to float this doll (named Margarita) up over the second-story balcony and scare the bejeezus out of the neighbors. When Margarita's psi reaches about 200, I start gritting my teeth in anticipation of the explosion (and probably for other, now involuntary, reasons). Someone whispers "Valium" in my ear and hands me a pill. Then it happens: A deafening pop, and pieces of latex vagina and plastic mouth fly around the room. I take the pill.

My ears are ringing and will continue to do so for the next three days.

2249h—Dancing Machine

Having fished all of the pieces of Margarita's plastic genitalia from my hair, Mischief and I go back to the nightclub and soon are dancing to '70s funk. Well, I'm dancing. She is writhing.

Strippers who have been strippers for a while can't really dance. They get so used to swinging from brass poles and grinding and undulating and what not, that they seem to forget how to actually dance on a dance floor in a public place. But this isn't exactly a public place, and I don't really mind the writhing, and at some point, she takes off her overworked shirt and we are pretty much the center of attention on the dance floor. But now the Valium is kicking in and I'm having trouble doing much more than writhing myself.

"You need a lap dance," she says.

I sure as hell do.

She sits me on one of the club's many couches and says she'll be right back. She returns, pulling Summer along behind her. Mischief sits next to me and Summer writhes on both of us. Soon everybody is licking everybody else's nipples and a gaggle of single guys stare from the bar. It can safely be said that I am now swinging. Wheeeeeeee!

2303h—Come Hither

Mischief walks/carries me back to Room 136. The Valium is amazingly strong. I'd rather be in her candle-filled love den, but she seems adamant about using 136. Mischief and I hoover another huge line of speed and she starts taking off her clothes. Three guys already have coagulated outside and are standing there expectantly. I lock the door and close the curtain. Summer can fend for herself.

0302h—Xanax and gack and ants, oh my

It is three in the morning and I am killing ants in the bathroom of Room 136. After two hours of unholy (in some states, illegal) sex, we both popped a few Xanax. She passed out and started snoring almost immediately. Hours later, here I am, gacked out of my brain and killing ants like it's my job. More Xanax.

0933h—The Cock Crows

I wake up semirested, teeth clenched, naked, and wrapped in my plastic sheet. Hard-core porn emanates from the TV. Mischief is gone.

0947h—Checkout

I pull on my pants and journey over to the hot tub before I check out. About a dozen other partygoers are basking naked in the morning sun, drinking mimosas. The group is very quiet, and I get the feeling none of them have slept. No one speaks. I ask about Mischief.

"She was out here a while ago, but her boyfriend came and picked her up."

Ouch.

"She said to tell you to be here tonight . . . she's got some surprises for you."

It is then, there, in the calm and cool of the morning, that I finally see the hot tub. Its waters are calm, even stagnant. It looks like egg-drop soup. Were a female to get into this tub, she would be pregnant inside of a minute. "They chlorinate it every Wednesday morning," someone says.

Memories of the previous night filter back into my head, and for the first time in about 20 years, I feel like I should go to church. I want to take a bath.

But not here.

The Great Italian Magazine Swindle

I slept for three days once I found my way back to my apartment from the Edgewater West. It was, as usual, my phone that woke me up later that week. In the sleepy seconds as I listened to the ring, it occurred to me that I was caught in a horrible, never-ending cycle, very much like a snake eating its own tail. The phone rings me awake to offer me jobs that I must take both to pay for the apartment I'll need to crash in after I get back from the previous assignment and to keep the phone on so that it can wake me up again, and so on, and on, and on, ad infinitum, ad absurdum, ad nauseam. I don't know whether it was the various chemicals still making the rounds in my circuitry, or the remnants of exhaustion, or sheer stupidity, but this really bothered me. Perhaps if I didn't answer the phone, I wouldn't get sent on God-knows-*what* kind of freakish and self-destructive fact-finding mission for whomever, only to collapse when finished, only to be awakened once again by the damn phone. I was so lost in this concentric circle of thought, so close to the sort of breakdown that typically results in previously balanced people saying "fuck it all" and moving to Montana to live in a toolshed filled with weaponry, that I didn't answer the phone. It was a pivotal movement, and if I had gone with it, just climbed aboard that train of thought and abandoned everything and hopped the Hound for Montana, everything might have been okay. But the more I woke up, the more I thought about things like plumbing and climate control and the convenience of not having to stalk and kill each meal, I decided I wasn't ready to go Back to the Land just yet. No. Wake up. Stand up. Back on the Dreadmill for another sprint through hostile territory until capture or collapse.

I have to listen to the voicemail four times before I can understand it. At first, of course, I suspect it is Boochie in rare form, drunk, on animal tranquilizers, having gargled with Anbesol, and talking in a bad accent with a mouthful of tampons. But, after careful analysis, this is not a *bad* accent, only a thick one. *Very* thick.

> *Yes, escoosah . . . thees ees Powwwwwwwwlo Picozziniti ate thee Sane Frahnceesco ohffice ove Gruner und Jarr Mondadori ahnd eef thees ees thee Jayesone Gahllahway dat wrote de 'Die-ry ove thee Viahgrah Feeeeeend', we would bee eentrested een toking weeth you abowwwt publishing thees story een owwr new mahgahzine . . . eef thees ees daht same Jayesone Gahllahway would you plees call me at _____. Eef thees ees not daht Jayesone Gahllahway, plees aksape my apologees. Grazie.*

Ah *shit!* This story just will not die. It won't leave me alone. Like a ghost from the grave of a corpse I had violated, this story was *haunting* me. *I hate it I hate it I hate it!*

But still . . . let's think about this . . . the story is already written. The evil is already out there. I already had been passed the eternally stiff Viagratic Torch from Bob Dole on prime-time TV. This Paolo guy sounds like he just wants to give me more money for something I already had done, pay me for suffering already incurred. What a fine idea. Of course, there is always the possibility that he is full of shit. But even if he is, he can't possibly be any worse than the Antichrist. Yeah, why not? I'll roll the dice. How can I lose?

"*Pronto?*"

"Paolo, this is Jayson Gallaway returning your call."

"Jayyyyyeesone, my good friend . . . thanke you soh mahch for cahlling me bahck."

And for the next three minutes, through an accent as thick as 10-cheese lasagne, in a dramatic monologue that consists almost exclusively of the sounds "ee" and "ow," Paolo explains his plans. His scheme was grand, indeed.

The largest publisher in Europe was launching a new magazine that was, to hear Paolo tell it, going to take over the world. Not a men's magazine, not a women's magazine, but a magazine for everyone. And what was the secret formula for global success? "Great stories . . . *lots* of pictures." I was dubious, but if this guy's enthusiasm was any indicator, perhaps they really thought this *could* be huge.

But I didn't *want* huge. Not for *that* story. I told Paolo (as I had told so many people by this point) that I had some other simply bitching stories that had nothing to do with erectile dysfunction or drugs. And like so many others, he was adamant: It was the Boner Story or nothing.

For a moment, I felt defeated. Another cruel and brutal

euchre. But then, slowly, a new feeling . . . strength. Confidence. Leverage. *Power.* I had never been in this position before. Sure, I wanted money, but I really wanted this story to go away. This magazine was not going to be published in America, and I was in no particular hurry to become Boner Boy over in Europe. It was then that I entered into the delicate diplomatic dance of negotiation.

"Ten thousand dollars. American."

Silence on the line. But he didn't hang up.

As Paolo thinks about this, let me take the opportunity to point out that asking for 10 grand for a short story that has already been published by an author no one has heard of, particularly when that story's central theme is genitalia, is rather like trying to get $500 for a used "back massager" at a garage sale. It simply doesn't happen. But Paolo hasn't hung up yet. Perhaps he's gone into shock.

"I'll need to cahll you bahck."

Holy shit! He's seriously considering it. *Ten grand!* That's like three month's rent in San Francisco. I'll be able to tell the Antichrist to go piss up a rope. Hell, I can *buy* his shitty magazine, and fire him, and *then* tell him to go piss up a rope, right after he lights *my* 10-foot bong.

Except that he doesn't call back. An hour goes by and he still hasn't called back. I keep picking up the phone to see if it's been shut off. Nope. Dial tone. Paolo isn't calling back.

Damn! Why didn't I just ask for five grand?

Two hours.

Three hours.

Midnight. No call. I dispatch a bottle of wine and a few Ambien and a bowlful of Jamaica's finest.

As usual, I am awakened the following day about noon by the screaming ringing of the phone.

"Mmmhello?"

"Ciaooooooooow . . ."

"Hi, Paolo."

"So I toked to my bose een Firenze, ahnd we theenk for save-ral reesones, your amowwnt ees too high."

"Hmm," I snorted curtly, as if I took umbrage, but what else could be expected from dealing with Europe. Which, of course, was not the case at all. I was simply in shock that Paolo and company not only had not laughed openly at my "offer," but had taken it seriously. I am not used to being taken seriously, particularly by people to whom I don't owe money. So I played along, curious to see where this could possibly go.

"Becose you alraidy wrote thee story, ahnd beecose ees alraidy beeen published, we theenk thaht pairhaps a more reeleestic amowmt mide bee seex. Seex thowsand dohllars."

I try, I *really* try to maintain my "poker voice." Any semblance of a poker face was long gone as I sat there, eyes wide with disbelief, drop-jawed, trying to keep from both dropping the phone and offering to give Paolo a lap dance. *Six K! Fucking A!* I want to burst into song. Kick open the front door and start hollering glorious Negro spirituals. But I stayed cool, and let Paolo sweat for a second.

"Okay," I finally said, sounding balanced between disappointment and sincerity.

"Ake-sellent! My bose weel bee vahry happy. Now seence we are geeving you so mahch money, we wont to saind a photographer to take peeksures weeth you ahnd your girlfriend . . ."

Uh-oh. This was a problem—a big problem. Lolita had got-

ten all cheesed and given me the Finger right around the time
the story originally came out. Her screaming was incoherent
over the phone, but I think it had something to do with telling
the world about the Hello Kitty panties and such. I'm still not
sure what really happened, but I'm damn skippy she would not
be at all receptive to any contact from me, particularly if that
contact regarded a photo shoot with yrs. truly to promote the
same story. But I couldn't tell Paolo that.

"Um . . . well, Paolo, let me give her a call and see what her
schedule looks like, and I'll get back to you later."

"Bene, my friend. Call me dees aftairnoon or eevening."

Once again, I begin pacing laps around my apartment.
Once again, the woman downstairs starts in with her broom
handle. I begin marching and stomping, hoping she might find
the sound of goosesteps both familiar and soothing. Which evidently she does, because finally she stops already with the goddamn broom.

Shit. *Think!* All of the girls I know these days are strippers
or even deeper species of sex workers who, regardless of actual
age, look well over 19 by several years. Several *hard* years of
drug abuse and bad psychology and bar fights. No, no one eligible there. More pacing. More thinking. This was money I
desperately needed, and I could not blow it on my inability to
find a girl to pretend she was my girlfriend for a couple of
hours for a photo shoot with an Italian magazine. And Paolo
is expecting to hear back today. The time factor made the
situation desperate. Desperate times . . . desperate . . . *wait a
minute . . . isn't there . . .*

Rifling through piles of clothes waiting to be burned, I
finally find the phone book, and begin flipping frantically

through the pages. *Let's see . . . F . . . E . . . Electrical . . . Entertainment . . . Escorts . . .*

"Desperate Measures Escorts." A deep male voice.

"Hi . . . I have a special request."

"Most guys do."

"No, but really . . . I actually need an *escort,* not like, you know, a prostitute."

"Well that's good, sir, because we don't associate with prostitutes. That's why we're called an *escort* service."

"Yeah, yeah, yeah, whatever . . . but I'm *serious,* I actually need a girl to play the role of my girlfriend in a photo shoot."

"Yeah, listen, sir . . . it's okay. You don't have to justify anything to me. Call it whatever you want. What kinda girl you lookin' for?"

"All right, fine. She has to be eighteen or nineteen. She has to look young, but legal."

"You like 'em young, huh?"

"No, goddamnit, as a matter of fact I *don't* like 'em young. They pretty much just get in the way and piss me off when they're young. But this isn't about what I like, this is for a photo shoot requiring a girl who looks like she's nineteen years old."

"Okay, okay, settle down . . . I'm here to help. You sound familiar . . . have you called here before?"

"Never."

"Huh. Okay. Anything else?"

"Anything else what?"

"The girl . . . Black? White? Asian? Short? Tall?"

"Oh . . . yeah . . . good thinking. Um, well . . . white, I guess. And on the shorter side . . . say under five-five." And cute, you know? *Real*-looking. Like the sexy girl next door."

"Yeah . . . I've got a girl you might like. She's Italian . . . do white people think Italian is white?"

"Uh, sure, I guess, yeah."

"Her name is Celeste. She *real* cute. 'Bout five feet tall, big green eyes, blond hair down to the crack of dawn, you know what I'm saying? Cute feet. You like titties?"

"Does the Pope shit in the woods?"

"Cool, 'cuz this girl got some *titties.*"

"Sounds great. Do you have any pictures I can see?"

"Yep. Web site. Click on *Escorts* and click on *Celeste*. You'll like her."

"Okay . . . so how much is this going to cost?"

"Two-hundred-fitty dollars an hour. But if you want to take pictures or any other weird shit like that, she'll probably want extra."

"What do you mean, 'weird shit'?"

"You know, like . . ."

"Never mind. Is she available this week? What kind of notice do you need?"

"Yeah, she's available. We usually do like a day's notice. If you want to reserve her for a certain time, you'll probably want to put down a deposit, you know, just to make sure she doesn't go and make any other plans."

"Hmmm. Okay . . . I gotta call this magazine back and see when they wanna do this."

"A'ight, bro, whatever. Just holler when you ready."

I put down the phone and open my wallet. Forty-seven bucks. A bit short. Not good. I was going to have to get paid for the story up front, or at least get some sort of advance. I called Paolo.

"*Pronto?*"

"Hey, Paolo, it's Jayson Gallaway. *Como sta?*"

"Jayesone Gahlahway . . . Deed you ever notice your naim has thee saim number ove see-lables ass 'Ernaste Hame-ing-way'?"

"Um, no, actually I'd never thought about it like that."

"Ees true. He shot heemself een thee hade."

"That's the rumor. Listen, Paolo, I talked to my girlfriend."

"Deed she say 'yase'? Ees she achesited?"

"Oh, of course she is. She's *very* excited. But it's going to take a little effort to get her up here."

"Waat do you mean? Ware ees she?"

"Well, she's down in LA—she's a model, you know, and an actress, and she's very busy. She's actually under contract right now . . . it's very complicated."

"Hmmm."

"Yes. *Very* complicated. I think I can make it work, but I'm going to need some money first."

"Wha? Why you need the money first?"

"Well, she's a very busy model . . . lots of work . . ."

"She's pretty, your girlfriend?"

"Of *course*, Paulo . . . she's *Italian.*"

"Ahhhhh . . . you have fine taste, my friend."

"Thank you. Thank you. So anyway, yes, she's in the middle of a movie and some other stuff, so we need to fly her up here for this photo shoot."

"Thees should't be deefeecult . . . plane teeckets are cheap right now. How much are plane teeckets?"

"Well, I haven't really checked, but there's this other prob-lem . . ."

"Other problem?"

"Well, yes, like I was saying, she is under contract, so that while we're doing the photo shoot, we have to pay her agency a fee. It's all very complicated."

"You haf to pay your girlfriend a fee?"

"An hourly fee."

"Howerly fee?"

"Two hundred and fifty dollars. Per hour."

Silence on the line (it occurs to me that "Paolo Picozziniti" has the same number of syllables as "Benito Mussolini," but I suspect that right now is not the most opportune moment to say that, or anything else for that matter). Paolo was in Deep Think. I'm hoping that he will realize that he could hire some local model for about 75 bucks to do the shoot, but apparently the idea hasn't crossed his mind. I'd thought of doing just that before dialing Desperate Measures, but dismissed the idea immediately, certain that any legitimate modeling agency would laugh, openly *laugh* at a request from some freak looking for a teen-age girl for a supposed photo shoot with a supposed magazine that doesn't yet exist and oh yeah, by the way, the photographer and the magazine have to think that she's not a hired model but my actual girlfriend, and oh yeah, also, it's for a story about a Viagra Fiend. It wasn't that I feared laughter . . . I feared they might call the police. No. Too risky. Perhaps I should suggest the idea to Paolo . . . suggest hiring a "stand-in" for Lolita, but it seems important to him that this be my "real" girlfriend. I had been working for the likes of the Antichrist for so long, I was now genuinely surprised when confronted with things like ethics and integrity.

"Thees ess *cattivo,* thees fee."

"What is *cattivo?*"

"It means thees ees focking *bad!* Your chake ees coming from Firenze, so eet weel bee weeks before you gate it."

"Well, then, I guess we'll wait a couple of weeks."

"Oh, but wee cahn't."

"Oh, but we must. I don't have that kind of money laying around."

"Cattivo . . . cattivo . . . We half to do thees thees week."

Paolo was back in Deep Think. But not for long.

"Okay . . . I'll geev you a chake for feefteen hondrade dole-ars, and you pay me bahck wane you get your chake frome Firenze."

Holy shit yet again. This guy was going to loan me money, like, out of his personal bank account. I almost felt bad. Almost.

"That would be great, Paolo! Thank you so much! *Grazie.*"

"Prego, prego. Jus' be shoor you pay me bahck wane you get your chake."

"Of course, Paolo, you have my word."

Which he did. I've seen *The Godfather.* I still have night-mares about finding a horse's head in my bed.

That call done, there still were arrangements to be made.

"Desperate Measures Escorts."

It was the same guy I had spoken with earlier.

"Um . . . hi, I called earlier about a girl for a photo shoot, and you recommended Celeste?"

"Yeah . . . hey, how you doin', bro?"

"I'm good, thanks. So, yeah, I wanted to book Celeste for a few hours on Thursday afternoon."

"Cool, cool. You check her pics?"

"Yeah. She's cute." And it was true. Young looking, with big eyes that lent themselves to an appearance of naughty innocence. And though the photos had all been G-rated portraits, there had been visible and substantial cleavage. She was cute.

"Yeah, she fine. Wait till you get them titties all up in your face, dog . . ."

"Um, actually, like I was telling you before, this is for a photo shoot for a magazine, not for, you know . . ."

"Yeah, yeah, whatever. She got hella back, too, yo."

I no longer knew what he was talking about.

"Hella back?"

"Bootie. She got a nice big bootie."

"So yeah, anyway, we're going to do the shoot the day after tomorrow at noon, so I need her to get here about an hour before, so I can tell her how to . . . well, how to act like my girl-friend, I guess."

" 'Leven o'clock. Cool. Cash or credit?"

I fail to stifle a snicker. I just imagine some hooker-lookin' chick showing up with one of those big credit-card knuckle-busters, like department stores have, to imprint my credit card on a receipt, which I would save, of course, for tax purposes.

"I was just planning on paying cash."

"Tha's cool. What you may want to do, if you got a credit card, is give us that number, as, like, a deposit. Otherwise, you know, we can't really *guarantee* that she'll be available."

The stink of scam fills my lungs. About the last thing I want to do is give my credit-card number to some shady pimp across town at Desperate Measures Escorts. I didn't even want to give him my *name!* But given the man's tone, combined with my suspicious nature, I had reason to believe that any hesitation at this moment would be considered a "dis," and he would seize the opportunity to say, "I told you so, yo," or something like that, by sending some nasty, haggard bag of a transvestite out to the shoot. *Fuck it,* I thought. This credit card has been so far over its limit for so long that it really doesn't matter who knows the number. They'd have no more luck trying to use it than I'd had for the last year. But things turned unexpectedly ugly when I spelled out my name for him.

"Mother*fucker.*"

My knowledge of ghetto patois has significantly dwindled during the last decade, but even with my dulled sensitivity, this did not sound good.

"Um, is there a problem?"

"You goddamn right, there's a problem. You got my ass fired!"

"What the hell are you talking about?"

"This the same Jayson Gallaway got his dick stuck in somethin' and freaked out when it turned black?"

Whatever cool I had when this conversation started went right out the door, slamming it on the way out, dropping me directly into shock. Had he really just said what he'd said, or had I had some sort of rift in perception, a mutiny of the subconscious precipitating a breakdown? And if he had said it, how the hell was I supposed to answer? Say yes and admit to making one of the most woefully stupid mistakes of the 21st century involving one's own genitalia, and evidently incurring the wrath of the Unknown Pimp in extremis? But it would be moronic to try to deny it . . . to expect anyone to believe that there was another guy named Jayson Gallaway with the same spelling in San Francisco. No. I was doomed.

"Um . . . yeah?"

"This is Jerome, motherfucker. From the answering service. For your doctor."

"Oh shit."

"Oh shit is right, motherfucker. You got me fired over a fondue dinner! I don't even know what that is! What is it? Do you know?"

"Well, I think it's Swedish . . ."

"*Swedish!*"

"Um, yeah, and you can do it with chocolate or cheese, and . . ."

"Man, shut the fuck up! Fondue. I went to mu-fuckin' career college to get that job."

"Um . . . damn. I really don't know what to say, Jerome . . ."

"Well, you can start by not calling me fuckin' Jerome on the phone. My name for this particular entrepreneurial enterprise is Fuckemup G."

"How about 'The Artist Formerly Known as Jerome'?"

"How about I come over there and show you why they call me Fuckemup G?"

"No . . . that won't be necessary . . . not at all. Fuckemup G. No problem."

"A'ight den. You can also apologize."

"I am very sorry."

I wasn't sure at first, but a few seconds later, I definitely heard him laughing.

"'The Artist Formerly Known as Jerome.' I like that. Maybe I should just have a symbol."

"A big middle finger, maybe?"

"Yeah, one big-ass one-hundred-carat middle finger. I like it. Cool. Now let's handle this business."

"That's it? You're not gonna kick my ass?"

" 'S all good. You've redeemed your ass with this symbol

business. Besides, this b'nis is much more lucrative than takin' messages for some damn doctor."

"I can imagine."

"So you want Celeste, 'leven o'clock day after tomorrow. Gimme your address."

I did. Why not? Either he would kill me or he wouldn't. What the hell else was I going to do? Besides, it was for The Cause. At least that's what I kept telling myself that night every time I thought I heard something at the door.

The next day, the photographer Paolo had hired for the shoot woke me with a call. She seemed nice enough, but this was clearly not her typical assignment. Her forte was advertising and computer magazines. She seemed as uncomfortable with this assignment as I was, but for very different reasons.

"I really don't know what they want. I can't understand this Paolo guy. I just know they want some pictures of you and your girlfriend at a gas station, with you pumping gas and her looking at you in the rearview mirror, and then some pictures of the two of you at home, interacting."

I don't know if she hadn't read the story, or if she was just insecure, but she seemed to be looking to me for clarification. All I could give her was a warning.

"All I can tell you is that I hate having my picture taken. I mean, really, I *hate* it. It is traumatic to me. I've punched people for pointing cameras at me. So this isn't going to be easy for either one of us. Just go slow, and be patient, and tell me exactly what you want me to do, and hopefully this will go well."

She was reassuring, and for a few hours, I felt like this might somehow work out.

My contentment, however, was very short-lived. Things started going really fucking *cattivo* the following morning at seven, when this photographer called me back.

"Mmmhello?"

"Jayson, this is Diane, the photographer?"

"Hmmm-mmm."

"There's some breaking news downtown I've gotta work, so I'll be a couple hours late. I should be to your place about two or three this afternoon."

"Mmm-hmmm."

The panic attack began before the phone was even cradled.

Star 69 doesn't work. I call her home number but she is already gone. *Shit*. This was not happening . . . couldn't be.

I cut a Xanax in half and open a beer. I call Desperate Measures, but it just rings. I'm not surprised. Fuckemup G didn't really seem like a getting-up-early kind of guy. I was screwed. The only plan I could formulate was to just sit here and drink beer and wait for the feces to hit the fan, and hope I was quick enough to outrun the shit mist to follow.

1117h, there is a knock on my door. What stands before me when I open it is best described as a copy of a copy of a copy of a copy of the picture I had seen on the Web site when I clicked on Celeste, and by "copy," I mean the black-and-white kind you get for seven cents at Kinko's. I mean so distant from the original as to be barely related.

Celeste was missing at least one tooth, that I could see, in the front. Her complexion was the sort of thing you see in slide shows during eighth-grade sex ed, when they are showing you

victims of herpes and syphilis and other things to which you
and your mucous membranes should give a wide berth. And
then, there was the rest. Yes, she had very large breasts. Huge,
in fact. But whatever they brought to the party was invalidated
by the fact that despite their size, not even they could surpass
her gut, which in turn could not get over her hips, which were
outdone immediately by her thighs. I just stood there, somewhere between nonplussed and disgusted. She was chewing
gum, and after she shrugged as if to say, "Are you going to
invite me in, or what," she blew a bubble that, as it increased in
size, became increasingly lopsided in the area where her front
tooth should have been, but wasn't, thus allowing more gum
through to the bubble than the rest of her mouth.

"Celeste?" I asked sincerely. Perhaps there had been a mistake. Perhaps the girl in the picture had gotten a call from *Penthouse* or some such thing and had to run off, and sent her
stepsister, who had just gotten back from two years in the Peace
Corps cleaning feces in a leper colony and hadn't yet had a
chance to take a shower.

"That's me, baby. You wanna get this party started?" she
says, whistling during "this" and "started."

God *damn* Photoshop. God damn it to hell.

I usually have trouble being blunt, but having had a
healthy breakfast of Xanax and beer, combined with the sort of
edge had by people accustomed to numerous panic attacks
before noon, I stepped out into the hall and closed my door
behind me.

"Listen, I don't really know how to say this, but this just
isn't going to work. This is for a photo shoot for a magazine,
and . . . you just don't look like the pictures I saw. Don't get me

wrong . . . you look great. But you're just not what I need for this shoot."

"That's okay, sweetie. Just gimme my five hundred and I'll be on my way."

"Your five hundred what?"

"Dollars. G told me this would take a couple hours . . . that's five hundred. He gets half, I get half."

"Yeah, well, it *would* have been a couple hours, but . . . well, you don't look like you're supposed to look."

"Yeah, well, whatever, I just need to get paid and I need to pay G."

The panic attacks were coming at an amazing rate: one every four or five seconds. My heart felt like a grenade that had its pin pulled just before being placed in a paint-can shaker.

"All right, look," I said, pulling out my wallet, "here's your two-fifty. That's for you. I'll call . . . G . . . , and straighten things out with him."

She blew another lopsided bubble, let it burst over her herpetic lips, and sucked it loudly back into her mouth. She took the cash, tucked it into her cleavage, and then looked me up and down, slowly, and then laughed.

"*You* are gonna straighten things out with *him?* I'd like to see that." She started heading down the stairs.

"Sorry for the misunderstanding," I said, more to myself than to her.

"Whatever, dude . . . I'm bouncin'."

1129h. I dial the phone.

"Desperate Measures Escorts."

"Hey, uh . . . Fu . . . Jerome, what do you want me to call you? Fuck? Fuckem?"

"Call me G. How you doing? Is that bitch late?"

"No G. Well, yeah, she was a little late, but that's not the problem."

"There's a problem?" His tone was suddenly disturbingly calm.

"Yeah. She looks *nothing* like those pictures on your site."

"That's not true. Don't lie, brother. She looks a *little* like them pictures."

"I need another girl."

"Another one? I don't think Celeste is into the lesbian thing. Put her on the phone."

"No, not another girl as in 'in addition to.' Another girl as in 'instead of.'"

"Put Celeste on the phone."

"She's not here. I sent her back."

"Sent her back? This ain't Nordstrom's, motherfucker. You can't just send shit back saying it don't fit."

"But she *didn't* fit. She couldn't fit her fat ass through the door."

"I told you she got hella back. So, where'd she go?"

"I don't know. She *needs* to go to the free clinic."

"She's got acne . . . what's a girl gonna do?"

"Listen, G, I need your help. You've gotta hook me up with a girl. A good-looking girl. 'Good looking' being defined here as slender, weight-proportionate. As in she only should be a quarter as wide as she is tall. Here's the key . . . I'm five-eleven, one hundred seventy-five pounds. She can't weigh more than me, particularly if she's half-a-foot shorter than me, which she is supposed to be. She needs to have all of her teeth. She needs to have a full head of real hair. And she needs to look like she's about nineteen years old. And she doesn't need 'hella back' or hella anything. And she needs to be here in about an hour."

"You pay Celeste?"

"I gave her two-fifty. She wanted five hundred, but that's not happening. That was false advertising, and you know it. This is business. I know you understand that."

I could not believe what I was saying. I tried to stop myself, but it all just came out. Extreme pressure will do that to a person, I've found. And while I sounded like a badass, I was scared shitless. I was imagining Samuel L. Jackson coming by later in a black suit and tie to quote dire Bible passages before shooting me.

"You don't owe me a thing, G; I know that. I'm just in a bind and I'm thinking you can help me. If you can, I'll treat you right."

"You bet your ass you'll treat me right. Yeah. I can help you, but it's gonna cost you."

I didn't want to, but I had to ask.

"How much?"

"Thousand."

I had no fight left. None.

Well, maybe just a little.

"Okay. A thousand. But flat. No hourly rate. And if she doesn't look right, the deal's off. She doesn't get shit. No two-fifty. Nothing. I don't have time to waste."

G seemed to respect this.

"Gimme an hour. I'll get Athena."

"Is she cute?"

"No. Athena is perfect. Gimme an hour."

Click.

1327h. Big knock at the door. This whole thing had gotten

so out of control so long ago that I no longer had any room for
fear. The idea of getting shot sounded like a pleasant break
from this weirdness. I opened the door.

" 'Sup, Jayson . . . I'm G."

G extended his huge hand and I shook it. He released without breaking my wrist or yanking me out into the hallway.

"This is Athena."

I was speechless. She really was perfect. At least as close to
perfect as a young girl who is too attractive for her own good
can be after a night of clubbing. But she didn't look tired at all.
Her last dose of Ecstasy had been recent, I suspected.

"Come on in," I said to both of them.

"I came along just to make sure there were no more 'misun-
derstandings.' That, and Athena here can't really drive right now."

The three of us sit down and I give them the deal. Athena
has trouble keeping up, and G takes her into the bathroom.
There are snorting noises, and when they emerge, Athena is
much more focused. She gets the idea. We don't have time to
work out the details though, because Diane, the photographer,
knocks on the door.

Diane is a future soccer mom waiting for the right junior
account exec to sweep her off her pedicure. I introduce Athena
as my girlfriend and G as my friend. Athena amazes me. She
actually can act. She extends a hand to Diane.

"It's good to meet you, Diane. Nice to have you here."

Though she had sounded nice on the phone, Diane is not
my kind of person at all. We get off to a bad start when she
starts rearranging my room without asking. She takes down my
carefully hung drapes. "Natural light is the best light."

"Okay, let's do the shots here first, and then we've got to do the gas-station shots. So, what they want are some shots of the two of you in bed."

"Okay," I say nervously, leading Athena over to the bed and sitting on it. I lay back on my elbows and Athena lays her head on my chest. I'm impressed. She's doing well.

Diane looks at us like we are kindergarteners denying complicity in some school-yard wrongdoing.

"Is that how you guys sleep? You wear all of your clothes when you go to bed?"

"I sleep naked, Diane, but I'm not getting naked for these pictures."

"Well, just get down to your underwear."

Athena has no problem with this and begins removing her clothing, looking as if she had been yearning to shed a layer or two. It is an amazing process to watch, but I can't enjoy it, because, well, I hadn't planned for this at all.

"I don't *wear* underwear," I say. Because I don't.

"Well, just put some on," says Diane, without looking up from loading her camera.

"I don't have any. Why would I have underwear if I don't wear underwear?"

Now, she looks up from her camera.

"You mean you really don't wear underwear?" Diane cannot fathom this.

"That's kinda sexy," says Athena, who, clad in bra and panties, is now playing with my hair in a most distracting way.

Fuckemup G is laughing in the corner.

"How about some sweats? Do you have sweats?"

I go to the closet, grab some black sweat pants, and go into the bathroom to put them on. While I'm in there, I gargle with mouthwash and look in the mirror. I have a Moment. You know those moments? The ones when you're in your bathroom and in the other room is a mountainous pimp whose first name is Fuckemup; a teenage call girl who makes more money in a month than you will make all year is in your bed wearing nothing but a chemical grin and a very expensive bra and panty set; and a Nazi photographer sent by some Italian magazine that doesn't actually exist yet is there to take pictures of the whole scene? Yeah. One of *those* moments. It just doesn't get any weirder. Until you go back out into the room, and the photographer springs her next idea on you.

"They want you to put something in your pants to make it look like you've really got something going on down there."

G howls.

"What do you mean, 'make it look like I've got something going on down there'? I've got plenty going on down there."

"I wanna see," says Athena. I appreciate the sentiment, but she's supposed to be my longtime girlfriend, not some curious newcomer. I shoot her a look. She makes an "oops" shape with her admirable lips and smiles in a way she has obviously learned will get her forgiven by anything with a penis, regardless of the offense.

"No, that didn't come out right," rushes Diane, trying to remove her foot from her mouth, and trying to keep mine out of her ass. "What I mean is that they want something just ridiculous. Like absurd. Campy. Like this."

She hands me her plastic juice bottle. It is about 10 inches long and maybe two-and-a-half inches wide.

"You want me to put this in my pants?"

"It'll be great. C'mon, just do it. It'll be fun."

I do it. Athena sneaks a peek. There is fumbling. It is difficult, ironically enough, to arrange things so that the bottle will
stand up straight. Once Diane starts snapping pictures, Athena,
who obviously has had plenty of practice in front of cameras,
begins striking alluring poses and moving about. The slightest
movement causes the juice bottle to fall over suddenly, as if my
supposed erection has just been made to disappear by a magi-
cian in a sleazy lounge act. Each time it happens, Fuckemup G
laughs harder, until he literally is crying. He helps himself to
my bong, but I don't care about that or the laughter because
each time the juice bottle falls, Athena quickly grabs it and
readjusts it, manipulating other things in the process, and soon
the juice bottle is facing (Dare I say it? Sure, why not . . .) stiff
competition.

Diane is snapping away. Like two and three shots a second.
Athena is progressively getting more relaxed and into things.
The bottle keeps falling and more fumbling happens. G is
smoking like a chimney in Negril. And I snap.

"Okay, stop! Enough. Fuck this."

I reach into my pants and yank out the juice bottle and toss
it aside.

"No more pictures. We're done."

Athena looks at me like *What did I do,* and I lean over and
kiss her on the cheek.

"It's not your fault . . . this is just too weird." She smiles. I
turn to Diane.

"Diane, time to go. This just isn't working out the way I
thought. It's not my scene."

She looks at me with something just short of anger, as if I'm
being unprofessional.

"Sorry, Diane, but sticking a juice bottle down my pants was not what I had in mind here. We're done."

She is preparing to mount an argument, but G stands up audibly and says, "Time to go, Diane." Which is about the coolest thing in the world.

She packs up her camera gear and is gone within minutes. She doesn't say good-bye. Neither do I.

I give G the $1,550 left over from Paolo's advance. There are many reasons for this, not all of which I know at the time. Part of it is so he won't take Celeste's money, part of it is so he won't kick my ass here and now, part of it is for getting him fired from his previous job, part of it is that he hasn't kicked my ass yet, and actually has been a pretty cool guy, and part of it is, well, Athena has shown no interest in leaving even though the shoot is over. She is still there, in bed, in underwear, looking like she really would prefer not to get up and get dressed.

G shakes my hand.

"Call me if she wants me to come pick her up." And he's gone.

I call Paolo and tell him the whole deal is off. He is pissed and disappointed, but I don't care.

"Just call Florence and tell them I changed my mind. Cancel my check and have them reimburse you for yours."

I take two Valium. Athena takes seven.

I love Valium, but this time around I wish it didn't have such powerful amnesiac qualities: I truly would like to remember every detail of the three days and nights we were together. I remember enough to involuntarily smile every time I think of her. And without the Valium, in the brutal light of sobriety, I probably would have freaked out each time her pager went off in the middle of the night and she slipped on something slinky and left for an hour or two and came back and counted cash on my bed. The dangerous temptation might have been to grab her and hold her and tell her she's better than this and she can stay here with me and I'll take care of her and oh shit I'm having *feelings* here and G will understand, I think . . .

But then my life would become just another one of Sting's lyrics, and, well, fuck *that*. I have enough headaches without having to add, "Put in overtime and spend buckets of money I don't have and exert Herculean amounts of energy to keep some high-maintenance sex worker from cheating on me" to my daily "To Do" list.

Occasionally, I'll see Athena on the cover of the local "adult" newspaper. My reflexes want to pick up a copy, just for posterity's sake, so I can pull it out in 50 years and show the grandkids: "And this . . . this girl was almost your grandma." But then I hear Sting screaming about Roxanne and think to hell with it. Because who needs to be reminded, eh?

Dancer in the Dark

His name now actually came up on my Caller ID as "Antichrist."

"Mmmhello?"

"What do you mean you're not leaving the house any-more?"

"It's a pretty simple concept, really."

"But you *have* to leave the house. How the hell else are you going to cover stories?"

"I'm not. I'm just going to write. I'm not a reporter, you know."

"Well sure, but *shit*. I think you're being a little extreme."

"No man; I'm being normal. It's everything Out There that's extreme."

"Somebody needs to smoke more marijuana."

"Nope. Dulls the blade."

"Indeed," he whispered, just before I heard his tell-tale lighter click, and then the now-familiar bubbling sound. Eventually, he exhaled.

"So, they had you put a juice bottle in your pants?"

"Can you believe it? Fuckers."

"But you still got the girl."

"For a hefty sum."

"Bullshit. That was a pimp tip."

"Whatever. What do you want?"

"Another story."

"I'm not leaving the house."

"You don't have to."

"Oh?"

"Nope. Just sit right there and type."

"Any particular subject?"

"Funny you should ask."

"No good can come from this. What?"

"Well, I've got some pictures of you . . ."

"With the fucking juice bottle? I'm so gonna sue."

"No. Not those pictures. Some others. You appear to be writhing around on a club stage, no shirt, plastic pants . . ."

"Ah shit. Where'd you get those?"

"Resources. So yeah . . . I just *know* there's a story in there."

"Many stories. But not ones I want to write."

"Three thousand words. Anytime in the next two weeks. Four hundred bucks. Pick it up any time. Or I can send it to you since you're not leaving the house anymore."

"Five hundred if you use the pictures."

"Done."

"I hope you choke."

"See you soon."

No, I wasn't into bondage, but yes, I was a dancer at a bondage club. And now, apparently, I was going to write about it. But not before I got paid. I trekked down to that awful office, grabbed my cash (The Antichrist no longer bothered promising big payments in the future. He didn't have to. He knew I'd do his stories for his pittance.), and did the story. To wit, goddamnit:

Mister Twister

One lonely San Francisco night, I wandered into a bondage-
themed nightclub looking for some good music, and walked
out with a job as a dancer. My descent into the weird world
of fetish would provide many solid and scholarly psycho-
anthropological conclusions regarding the human condition.
    To wit:

- Everybody looks better in the dark.
- Being onstage makes you attractive, even if you really are
  not.
- Females are very, very different from males.
- There are some seriously disturbed people walking around
  free in our society.

Night #1

It was a dark and stormy night. Literally. I was, as usual, dead
broke. I knew some people who worked the door at the Trocadero Transfer in San Francisco who told me the music they
played on Wednesday nights was right up my proverbial alley
and never mind that it was a bondage club—there were really
cute girls with complex hair and tight plastic clothing there.
And I could get in for free. Free is good. So off I went into a
night that would change my life forever (cue dramatic music).
    My first impression of the club: lots of smoke, lasers, and
torches. A chain-link fence surrounds the dance floor on three
sides. A glance to the right shows a girl removing her top and
putting her arm around a statue of a crying angel. She poses

this way while a guy with alarmingly greasy hair snaps her picture. She then nonchalantly replaces her top and the two head for the dance floor.

A very petite girl sidles up to the bar next to me, alone, forcing herself to appear like she is having the time of her life, although she obviously is not. I feel sorry for her, sort of, so I try to strike up a conversation, asking her name. This quickly gets far more complicated than it really ought to be. She doesn't speak a hell of a lot of English. After much verbal wrangling and screaming at each other over what seems to be an ever-crescendoing level of noise, it is established to some degree of clarity that her name is Yvi and she is an exchange student from Hamburg, Germany. I try to bring the dialogue to a quick close, but she has fingered me as a nice guy and wants to talk more. Our intercourse is, needless to say, somewhat problematic.

"So how long have you been in America?" I yell.

"Vhat?"

"How long have you been in America?"

God only knows what she says in reply, but I nod at her encouragingly like I hear and comprehend. She starts talking about something and seems to like whatever it is she is talking about because she keeps nodding and smiling excitedly. The truth is I can't hear a goddamn word she is saying. But I nod every few seconds and laugh when she does. She seems to get a lot of enjoyment out of the conversation.

Three potent cocktails having been dispatched, I head for the main room and circle the perimeter of the dance floor. It is very dark, both literally and sartorially. Everybody's hair seems to be bluish-black or some other color not occurring in nature. There are lots of fake breasts, especially on the women. Everybody is dressed in leather, lace, or plastic. And no one can dance. I mean, not really. Some of them know a few steps, but none of them seems to have any real sense of rhythm.

The dance floor is more or less surrounded by a catwalk where the "beautiful people"—the people who never pay the cover, the people the DJ calls every week to make sure they're going to show up, et cetera—dance. They are not so much dancing as writhing ecstatically. Four girls and one guy. Their respective dancing abilities (in my patently subjective opinion) range from okay to downright shitty. We're talking about them not only having no rhythm, which can be easily compensated for by looking really damn good, but also *no style whatsoever*.

I quickly decide that it would be in everyone's best interest if I just jumped onstage and did my thing.

I am up there a good four seconds before someone starts grabbing at my 14-hole Doc Martens. I look down to find a very attractive, heavily tattooed mulatto girl, wearing a tight plastic nurse's outfit (which, by the way, yowza), looking rather unappreciative of my efforts. Her mouth is moving, but given the Wagnerian volume of the music, looking down at her is like watching a soft-core porno with the mute on.

But she keeps tugging at my damn boot like it's her job (which, I was about to find out, it is). So I lean down to hear what she has to say, and she screams a line that (although I don't know it yet) I will find myself saying literally hundreds of times during the next two years: "You can't be up here—only dancers are allowed up here!"

Just what in the hell did she think I was doing, I ask her in slightly less severe terms.

"No," she shouts back, "it's for the *club's* dancers—the employees!"

You mean these—these—poseurs are getting paid? I couldn't believe it. Again, keeping in mind the cocktails, it should come as no small surprise that I, the normally shy guy who has never even asked a girl to dance, shout back with almost papal authority, "Why don't we call this an audition?" She looks annoyed, but then looks me up and down, slightly less annoyed, and says, "All right, *one song*."

Heh. I feel a sense of victory, however temporary. So, for the next three minutes I dance like a pyromaniac on fire. Evidently, I pass the audition. "My name is Colette," she says afterward. "I manage the dancers. Meet me at the bar in an hour and we'll talk."

So, in an hour, I find Colette and her lovely outfit holding court at the bar. She is, as one would expect, surrounded by admirers of both sexes, not only because she is attractive, but also because she is management. She has status in the club scene, and in the club scene, status is very important. She sees me and smiles. "I'm sorry about being so rude to you at first—I didn't know you wanted a job."

Neither did I.

"So here's the deal," she says. "I'll put you on the schedule. You'll be on every other week, $75 a night. Plus, you'll get a bunch of drink tickets you can use yourself or give to friends or whatever. Oh yeah, and you get to put two people on the guest list every week."

Hot damn.

Night #2

Gulp. It is with very mixed feelings that I drive to the club that second night. On the one hand, I feel pretty damned stoked. I am officially "cool." On the other hand, I now have contractual obligations to fulfill that include getting in front of a couple of hundred people while dressed in tight plastic clothes and savagely shaking my ass (among other things). While I know a lot of people do a lot more crazy things than that for a living, this was very new ground for me.

Colette introduces me to the girls, all of whom are very nice. As she puts on her clothes, she tells us where we are going to be "stationed" that night. I am to be on the main stage. Gulp again. So, at 10:30 p.m., we all climb to our respective perches and begin to shake our booties. It is a very strange thing, indeed, to find yourself on a stage in a bondage club with no shirt and a red spotlight shining down on you, and a whole bunch of jaded, cynical partygoers looking up as if to say, "Okay—so now what?" and to know that if you don't shake your ass now, well, bad things will happen.

So the next song starts and I actuate my ass and I block out the couple of hundred people in front of me and in about 45 seconds, I am having the time of my life.

Anthropological Observation #1: Bondage flicks play on several monitors around the club. After a while, I am relaxed enough to sort-of watch them while I'm onstage. Amazing. There is no actual sex in these things. Just a whole bunch of people dressed like nightmares, wearing gas masks, spanking each other and binding each other's genitalia tightly until they turn all colors of the rainbow. But no sex.

The time flies. At one in the morning, Colette comes by and tells me I did an incredible job and hands me an envelope full of money and asks me if I can come back the following week; she's going to fire the other guy.

Sure, I say. And with that I head up to the sweaty, naked dressing room with three girls.

After toweling off and putting on street clothes, I come down just in time to catch the infamous announcement the DJ makes every night at closing, which goes like this: "If you are not working here or sleeping with someone who works here, you must get out now." I am hanging out simply because I can, when I see a minor squabble occurring near the bar. It is Yvi. She is arguing with one of the bouncers and pointing with emphasis at me. He turns around and looks at me: "Is she sleeping with you?" I am the definition of nonplussed. "Sure," I say. Why not?

That was the first night of many that I would disappoint the hell out of some girl who assumed that because I was onstage at a bondage club, I was (a) some sort of porn star, (b) the owner of some absurd array of sadistic torture devices and love toys, and/or (c) single and available.

The boring truth is that I have never been in a porno. I'm not at all into bondage and find the people who are a little odd. Don't get me wrong, I enjoy being handcuffed by a loved one as much as anyone else—every once in a while. But whips and chains and leather masks with zippers where the mouth should be are a bit over the line for me. And, I had a girlfriend during my tenure as a dancer, to whom I was very faithful.

Personal Observation: A heterosexual male dancer does not get as many offers for anything resembling "normal" sex as one might think. Here's what I mean. The female dancers with whom I worked almost always had to have a bouncer nearby, because inevitably some jackass who'd had a few too many would come up and proposition carnal acts or attempt to grope, etc. Not so in reverse. Where guys will approach a female dancer and just lay (as it were) everything right out there in the open, girls just stare. *Not once* did a girl come up and proposition me. They would stare. I would see a girl maybe 40 feet away, leaning up against a rail, staring directly at me for hours. But they would never approach.

Occasionally, those under the influence would sidle up and smile chemically, but if I so much as looked or smiled back at them, they would giggle and run off. Over the years, I was approached by a few men who wanted things as varied as my participation in a gay bachelor party to watching me have sex with their wives, which wives, by the way, if they were there as well, stayed a good distance away and waved eager acknowledgment when their husbands pointed them out.

None of these offers was accepted.

So, on nights when a girl would sort-of latch on to me, basically because there was no one else to latch on to, and find herself with no place to go and no way to get there even if there was, I would, in a very Christlike gesture of compassion, take in a stray or two. Or three. Yvi was such a case. She stayed at my apartment for three days until her flight back to Hamburg. She was a very nice girl and I think pleasantly surprised to find I was a very nice, normal guy with a graduate degree who just had an unusual job. Others were not quite so understanding.

Night #7

I know that saying you go to a bondage club because of the good music is tantamount to claiming your subscription to *Hustler* is for the insightful articles. But it was true in my case.

Yet, I was finding myself unwittingly getting more and more immersed in the bondage scene.

The Bay Area is home to a thriving and surprisingly large bondage/fetish/S&M community. On any night of the week, Joe Masochist can find two or three well-organized events to attend. And, as sort-of "ambassadors" of pain, the dancers with whom I was working and I would go to some of these events to hand out flyers and flirt with people, in order to try to drum up new business for the club. As I said before, I was not into bondage to begin with, and after visiting that culture for a while, I was into it even less.

Real bondage clubs (not like the club where I was dancing, which was a centrally located, very public nightclub with a bondage theme) are very spooky places. Imagine the Gimp scene in *Pulp Fiction* mixed with Jame Gumb's basement in *The Silence of the Lambs* and you're on the right track. Every one I went to was, it seemed, a dark, cavernous place. Cold, emotionless techno music pounds from unseen sources in every room. In addition to the absence of real light, there also is the transgender factor. Most of the men you see are men, but many of the women you see are men as well. And there are some creatures that simply defy categorization: Stunning supermodel types who are seven feet tall in their heels, with voices a good octave deeper than mine; unearthly "she-hes" to whom not even the term "hermaphroditic" applies. There also are people you just know have lengthy criminal records, with crappy blue-and-black prison tattoos, who obviously ceased taking their professionally dispensed medication some time ago and now here they are, dressed up horrifically and looking for love or the next best thing.

I attended the first of these gatherings with an attractive dancer who calls herself Zoe. In the cab on the way there, I studied the flyer for the event. It made me want to go home and pull the covers up over my head: "Hide-bound hell! Bitches gag, choke, and beg for forgiveness from our masters. See you on the second floor, dungeon brats! Whip-snapping Doms ride, crop, and humiliate undeserving wimps! Their puny whimpering only inspires a vicious contempt and yet more severe punishment! Maggots submit! Cross-dressers, submissive men, ass-beatings, leather-lovin', dominant women, and amputees."

"Amputees?" I actually said that out loud in the cab. Zoe just laughed. "Yeah, they're a real trip."

Terrif.

We both are dressed completely in leather and plastic, with her motif being a schoolgirl from hell, complete with thigh-high patent-leather boots that climb up into a plaid skirt, a see-through top, and a dog collar with a leash that I employed to lead her around.

From the outside, this place looks like just another warehouse in a suburban industrial district, except for two menacing, leather-clad men standing outside the door, the dim light from inside providing scarcely more illumination than the streetlights. We step inside the makeshift "foyer" that has many supposedly inducing signs and promises of things to come (as it were). The most prominent reads, "No Pain, No Pleasure," which leads at least one person (that being me) to wonder: Then just what the hell are we coming here for?

We enter and have to sign the Contract Waiver. Everyone has to sign it. It is perhaps the most unusual document I've ever put my name to. By signing it, Zoe and I agree to:

- Not engage in unsafe sex with each other or anyone else we meet during the night. (The club had placed baskets of condoms, lubrications, gloves, Saran Wrap, alcohol—the sterilizing kind, not the drinking kind—and water pretty much everywhere around the premises.)
- Not touch anyone who does not want to be touched, and generally respect everyone's space and boundaries.
- Not exchange sex for money, drugs, or anything else.

And into the club we go.

In one room, people have signed up either themselves or the person(s) they have brought to be auctioned off to the highest bidder, with proceeds going to AIDS research.

The next chamber is a workout room, complete with free weights and various Nazi-looking Nautilus contraptions. This spot is very popular with the more "normal" section of the evening's demographic. There are a few strippers in regular clothes, looking like they just got off work, with their jock/bouncer boyfriends, giving lap dances to their jock/bouncer boyfriends on the weight machines. All rated PG-13.

Then we come to a very strange place indeed: another cavernous room, this one full of teepees. But the inhabitants of these teepees have nothing in common with the Indians of the Old West, save for the fact that they are not wearing a hell of a lot. The teepees (there are about 20 of them) are lit from the inside. On some of them the flaps are closed, the occupants wanting at least a modicum of privacy.

Finally, we come upon a teepee where the flap is open, revealing a very adipose man who actually does have a Native-American cast to him, naked as the truth, and posing languidly,

as if expecting someone to come in and have some sort of
porno powwow with him. Maybe smoke his peace pipe.

As Zoe and I proceed further into the darkness, it becomes
evident that this place is set up rather like Dante's Inferno, each
level we descend more dark and spooky than the last. After
we've successfully navigated the Carnal Frontier, we proceed
down a flight of stairs, into what could easily pass as de Sade's
Day Care Center. I grip Zoe's leash tightly as we carefully wander through the darkness. She runs into a photographer from a
local adult newspaper and poses for several pictures.

Psychological Observation: I consider myself to be fairly
hale, mentally speaking. I don't have nightmares after watching
scary movies; I never felt any unnatural attraction to my
mother; and I never have done cruel things to small animals. I
don't spook easily. However, check this out: There was only one
amputee I saw that night, and I have a dark suspicion he was
corralled at the last minute by the organizers to fulfill the promises stated on their promotional flyers. Let me tell you, in my
few decades on this planet, I have seen NOTHING more genuinely disturbing than watching a man, obviously homeless,
sitting on a floor in a dungeon, leaning up against a wall, and
eating popcorn out of his prosthetic leg, which is propped up
next to him, while "people" of both sexes occasionally ask if he
will "nub" them.

As is typical with such events, only about 3 of the 100 or so
people I see naked should be naked (and one of them is Zoe).
All in all, though there are definitely some interesting sights to
behold, it is not a whole hell of a lot of fun. Emerging from the
depths of the dungeon and stepping back onto the civilized
streets, I find myself feeling as if I've been rolling around in the

sewer. And I'm looking at people suspiciously. And I will never be able to eat popcorn again.

Night #15

As is the case with every nightclub, the one where I danced was kept afloat by its "regulars," patrons who would attend each and every week, regardless. It could be Christmas Eve—these people would be there. In fact, I can guarantee you that several people who were regulars long before I even moved to the Bay Area can still be found there this week.

One such regular (it seems funny to use that term to describe some of the most irregular people I had ever met) was known as Boot Boy. I first met Boot Boy by kicking him in the ribs. One night, as I was walking to the bar during a break to get a bottle of water, one of my heavily booted feet came into hard contact with a substantial mass of protoplasm on the floor. Now, before I tell you what he was doing, let me tell you just a little bit about the floors of nightclubs. They are not clean. They have been trod upon, danced on, sweated on, puked on, bled on, snot-rocketed on, et cetera, ad nauseam, ad infinitum. They are miasmic. There are grates on the drains of showers in state prisons that are cleaner than the floors of nightclubs.

That having been said, I looked down with some surprise to find a person, apparently male, in a sort-of vertical fetal position, that of extreme supplication. He apparently was too engrossed in his present activity to give much of a damn about the unintentional kick to the ribs I had just given him. The engrossing activity was that of licking, passionately and thoroughly (we're talking about even the soles), the shoes of a very pulchritudinous goth chick. Now, I would imagine this sickness to at least be taken by its recipient as a form of extreme flattery. This girl hardly acknowledged Boot Boy's presence. In hindsight, maybe she didn't know he was down there. But she had to, because he had a killer grip on her boot and was really licking the hell out of this thing. As my tolerance for weirdness already was geographically higher than most people from working in this club for so long, I didn't pay that much attention to it. I got my water and stepped carefully over him as I headed back for the stage.

Turns out that Boot Boy was a very regular irregular and everybody knew him. He was a decent-looking guy, normal in a Jeffrey Dahmer sort of way, who would go around to all of the girls in the club and ask them politely if he could lick their footwear, in much the same manner as other, more traditional males ask if they might buy a woman a drink. A lot of women told him to go jump, but many allowed him to do so, some rather tolerantly, others downright enthusiastically. By all accounts, the guy was totally harmless and sincerely just wanted to lick women's footwear. His lingual salutes never were followed by sleazy segues, either subtle or blatant, for sex. He just wanted to lick chicks' shoes. One night, I was walking Zoe to her car and she brought Boot Boy along with us. Zoe essentially lived out of her car, crashing wherever, and so had most of her worldly belongings in her trunk. Among the myriad of oddities in there were several pairs of worn-out stripper heels and patent-leather boots. Speaking from experience, the shoes of a dancer are not something to be hungered for in any way, on any level, in any sense. But Boot Boy was willing to shell out $60 for four pairs of Zoe's old boots, and

God only knows what the hell he did with them once he got them into the privacy of his sanctum.

Night #23

They say that whatever you are doing when the clock hits midnight on New Year's Eve is what you will be doing for the rest of the year, more or less. The previous year, I was alone and drunk, and that was the way the year flowed, for the most part. So, it was with ferocious excitement that I looked forward to being onstage, half-naked, and being ogled by a bunch of cute, drunk women, when the midnight moment arrived.

I hit the stage at exactly midnight. There was supposed to be some sort of balloon drop, but it didn't come off at the precise moment, so a bunch of bouncers armed with sticks and broom handles beat the contraption like a piñata until it broke and the balloons rained down.

At about two in the morning, a girl appears at the foot of my stage, staring directly up at me, her face almost parallel to the ground. She looks reasonably attractive at that angle, in that light (see Anthropological Observation #2 below), which is good, because she makes it rather obvious that she really doesn't want to be anywhere in the world but right there. God only knows what she's on, but it seems to be giving her the uncanny ability to stare at me for 15 minutes without blinking. Soon she is stroking my calf, which is not only impairing my ability to dance and putting her in danger of being kicked in the head, but is giving me a strong case of the creeps. I hand her about 53 drink tickets and send her toward the bar. I will regret doing so before the sun rises on this dark day.

Anthropological Observation #2: It is no accident that all nightclubs are very, very dark, and that the patrons of such clubs are encouraged to drink heavily. People, on the whole, look better in the dark and through eyes that are under the influence. The occasional flash of laser or strobe gives hints of another's appearance, but really notable physical faults, blemishes, or absences are easily hidden in such an environment. It is, conversely, no accident that the quickest way to clear out a club at the end of the night is to turn on all of the house lights, revealing in all their fluorescent horror the true appearance of the person with whom one was just considering copulating.

Okay, four in the morning, January 1. There's the DJ: "If you do not work here or sleep with someone who does, you need to leave now." On come the lights. As people clear out quickly, I see a bouncer helping the girl to whom I gave the drink tickets down the stairs. She is in what used to be called "a bad way."

"This one belong to you?" he asks.

Her eyes sort of open and she straightens slightly with recognition: "You take me home."

The phalanx of cabs that had been waiting with anticipation outside the club has been quickly depleted. She is alone, barely vertical, and quite obviously without the ability to get home. The bouncer sort of lays her at my feet.

Shit.

Somehow I get her in my car and ask her where she lives. She leans the seat back.

"The Mission," she says. "Drive to Nineteenth Street."

About halfway there, she pulls up what I suppose is technically a skirt, revealing a surprisingly tasteful and minimalist choice in G-strings. Red, heavy on lace, while not really being heavy on anything. And just like that it is pulled to the side and she begins moaning and doing R-rated things. Then X-rated things. I almost wreck the car three times in one block.

"Pull over," she starts moaning. "Pull over now." For a second I think maybe she's going to be sick, but what she does next makes it clear that she's feeling just fine. And then it happens. She passes out. Cold. Dead weight. Great. It is 4:30 a.m. on New Year's Day; I am a white boy with dreadlocks in a really bad neighborhood with a dangerously naked girl, whose name I never knew, unconscious and horizontal in my car, and not even a slightly believable explanation to give the police if they were to stop me and ask questions. More attempts to rouse her. More failure. I have to take her to my house.

Into the bedroom she goes, removing her clothes (except for her boots) with surprising ease, and falling onto the bed.

"Come here," she moans sloppily.

"Nope," I say. "You're on the couch."

She is suddenly very, very sober.

"What? What are you? Some kind of fag?"

"Nope. Got a girlfriend. Who, by the way, would probably kick both of our asses just knowing you slept on the couch."

After a whole lot of bad static, I'm the one sleeping on the couch, exacting my vengeance in the morning when I wake her up at 8 a.m. and put her hungover ass in a cab.

Quitting Time

On an autumn night in 1998, when the Trocadero was being rented to a hip-hop radio station, an altercation ended with one guy shooting another guy in the chest. The city instantly revoked the Trocadero's after-hours permit, effectively closing it.

The bondage club moved to a different venue, Colette quit, and I became the manager, a position I held for about a year. Being manager entailed corralling dancers and cajoling them to be at a certain place at a certain time. A gross generalization here, but dancers and strippers tend, on the whole, to not be the most reliable people. Unless it's some prepaid bachelor party, your chances are, at best, 50–50 that a dancer-stripper will show up (if at all) on time to anything, including her own wedding.

Wrangling dancers is not a fun thing to do. One girl showed up after four consecutive absences, acting as if no transgression had occurred. She (and many others) slipped into this weird cutesy/flirty mode that most dancers or really attractive women (and men, I suppose) slip into, which allows them to think that sticking out their chests and blinking excessively will redeem them from all wrongdoing. No dice. And just so you know, dancers don't take rejection well at all.

Another aspect that killed off the fun factor was that my role as manager evolved into press liaison. Whenever it came time to do a feature on the hottest clubs of the Bay Area, or Weirdest Tourist Attractions, or whatever, the local press would send a photographer and reporter out to talk to us. Since the guys that actually ran the club kept a Masonic air of distance and secrecy around them (I didn't even meet them until I had worked there for a year), the reporters usually approached the dancers, who would point them to me. Got my picture in a few papers, but the comments were pretty minimal. What was I going to say? That I found most of the people here, at best, harmless and not even a fraction as interesting as the reporter was hoping, and, at worst, pathetic bootlickers who probably devoted a good portion of their nonclub time to role-playing games with other people who were old enough to know better? No. Even my dancing was becoming uninspired. What used to be my version of couch time and catharsis was, alas, becoming just another job. And that was no good for either the club or me.

And so, one day I quit. It wasn't even a good, honest quitting; I just didn't show up the next week or any other week.

The club is still open and I hear a variety of reviews about it, ranging from "It's pretty cool" to "It's sucked ever since you left. You should come back." I consider it sometimes, especially when I find myself at home on Wednesday nights like this one, alone, watching public-access TV and thinking that the cat box really needs to be cleaned.

The Art of Darkness

I had almost convinced myself to go to the club and get my dancing job back. Times were tough. I was broke, and my landlord was leaving notes on my door citing criminal codes. The Antichrist had been arrested for something heinous, and police were questioning his known associates. Things were getting desperate indeed, when the publisher of various well-known pornographic magazines with either impressive or disturbing (depending on your perspective) subscription statistics and having heady titles such as *Swank* and *Just 18* found me through e-mail and asked if I'd be interested in scribbling some smut for them.

"Why not?" I thought. And then my thought continued: "The Marquis de Sade built an entire career out of applying his sacred writing abilities to the profane world of salaciousness, and his legacy is eternal. His prose has been required reading in advanced-placement English classes in fine high schools for decades, and just this week I saw on the shelves of a local bookstore a new line of well-crafted pop-up books based on the high points of the Marquis's massive oeuvre."

Why not, indeed.

After I responded positively to their initial e-mail, the prenominated pornographers sent me a multimedia collection of splendid indecency in the form of several magazines, a few low-quality Xeroxes of "erotic" photo layouts, and a video cassette with the intriguing title of *Young Muffs 3* crudely printed on a plain white sticker. This scandalous omnium-gatherum arrives in, as one might expect, a plain brown envelope, which is somehow *so* plain that its plainness overachieves and causes suspicion and sleaziness that would probably have been far less if they had simply printed *Swank* and the return address on a Day-Glo orange sticker. But there is no return address at all, adding to the too-plainness of the oversized brown envelope and giving the thing a sinister vibe. It's the sort of thing one would expect to receive a body part in if one were expecting to receive a body part via parcel post. Which I am not. Which is why I opened the thing instead of calling the police or whatever.

A closer examination of the envelope's contents reveals the glossy magazines to be one copy of *Swank* magazine ("HARD SEX PICS!") and one copy of *Just 18* magazine ("100% Rookie Nookie"), with Post-It slips marking sections of the magazines to which the editor evidently wants me to pay special attention. The relatively shoddy black-and-white copies of layouts (*sans* text) feature very young-looking models with relatively small breasts and pigtails, and absurdly childlike accoutrements (such as oversized lollipops and pacifiers). Each was in various and progressively extreme states of undress, with wide-eyed looks of innocently naughty surprise, performing sexual acts ranging from the incongruously perverse to the impressively athletic and even gymnastic, which acts serve to patently obliterate any illusion of innocence or purity established by the pigtails and lollipops and so on. At least it does for me. Not so, apparently, for the black-trench-coat crowd that makes up *Just 18's* target demographic. I set aside *Young Muffs 3* for the time being.

After continued examination of the items, I finally find a regular-sized Post-It note, upon which is scrawled my assignment. After much page-turning and brow-furrowing and three out-loud *"what the fucks,"* I finally am able to interpret the cryptic message: Watch *Young Muffs 3* and review it (presumably in the manner that other reviewers have used, which manner is exemplified by one of the Post-It strips in the copy of *Swank* I've been sent), and then write something called "set-copy," again exemplified in a Post-It-stripped page, this time in the copy of *Just 18.*

"Set-copy" is, in as much as I can make out after the aforementioned page-turning and so on, prose written from the approximated perspective of a very concupiscent, young, sexually inexperienced girl who somehow got coaxed into taking triple-X pictures with a lesbian lover or an overendowed male or by herself experimenting with a dildo that she just stumbled across in her older sister's drawer, etc.

I've attempted to write from a female perspective before, comfortably admitting to myself that I was unqualified to do so. But, as usual, what the hell? It might be an interesting exercise, and they are offering a nickel a word, so yeah, why not? How difficult could it be? It's just a matter of getting sufficiently into character and then letting the words flow.

The computer clicks and whirs as a new file opens and my bladder sends an urgent message to the Head Office: *Gotta pee.*

In the bathroom, I decide now is as good a time as any to get into character. Rather than pulling the lid and seat up for my typically masculine micturation stance, I leave the seat down, drop trou, and pee sitting down for the first time since I was four years old. When done, I have no additional insight into the female psyche. Damn. This might be more difficult than I originally thought. *Hmmm.* Perhaps I should review the movie first. *Young Muffs 3.*

Having, as usual, no idea what I'm doing, I pause the tape several times during the opening credits, hurriedly scribbling the names of people participating in this entertainment. The "stars" have predictably predictable names: Felony, Mia, Taylor, Amber, Luciano, Claudio, Mark Wood, and so on. It is worth noting that no one is given, or rather no one *takes*, directorial credit. In the cutthroat world of film, where no credit is too small for an aspiring director's or producer's résumé, I find the fact that no one wanted credit for this film a substantial review in and of itself. Nonetheless, I endure the next 90 minutes of tape in the name of artistic integrity (though it only takes me about 23 minutes as I quickly discover that if one watches the "introductory" segment of each scene, when the girl introduces herself and is asked a series of questions, and fast-forwards though the balance—which balance constitutes about 80 percent of the tape—one has "seen" the movie well enough to review it).

Just 18 wants 350 words. By the time I'm done, my review is more than 1,500 words, far longer, I can assure you, than any script that may ever have existed for the film. The shortened version went something like this:

> As you can imagine, this one is a little thin in plot. But who cares? In Young Muffs 3, you'll find six very bad girls, all with

tattoos and piercings and a surprising amount of carnal talent for only being 18 years old.

Things get rolling with Felony, a gorgeous girl who never takes off her socks and has a tongue piercing that says "Pimp" on it. She smokes, she likes pretty much everything and everyone, and her favorite position is doggie. Every shot of her getting pussy-fucked also shows an asshole so inviting it should say "RSVP" with a phone number on it. And sure enough, her well-hung costar eventually aims for the two-hole and Felony takes it all like a champ. Nice!

Next up is Mia Starr, cute in an illiterate, trailer-trash sort of way. Don't get me wrong—she's not the type of girl you'd kick out of bed—unless there was room on the floor. Nothing too special about this scene in terms of sex, but there is something about Mia I can't put my finger in . . . I mean on . . . I can't put my finger on.

Taylor McCay is a girl in pigtails who looks and acts a lot like "Rollergirl" in Boogie Nights. She responds well to commands and seems to have a good time. Her talents are many, but especially noteworthy is her oral prowess.

Then there's Julia, a girl who seems legitimately confused about getting roped into a threesome with a couple. The look on her face throughout the scene is that of a virgin on prom night. Her biggest concern about her performance in this movie is that her mother will find out. Yowza.

And that brings us to Priscilla Jane, a girl who makes this whole movie worthwhile. In fact, she makes the world a better place to be. She has nice breast implants, a pentagram necklace, and wants nothing more out of life than to have two guys at the same time. Sure 'nuff, two guys are procured: Both have

big dicks, bad attitudes, and say things like, "I'm gonna give
you all the self-confidence you'll need to fuck all the guys in
the neighborhood . . . because that's all you're good for!"

    Any flick that ends with a teen girl covered in jizz, looking
into the camera and saying, "Hi, Mommy," is worth checking out.

I felt like I had been rolling around in a sewer after writing it,
but that was the job. Having said that, when the review is published, I am upset by a few things. The first is that the magazine
has taken the liberty of giving the movie a rating of four cherries.
Just 18, for reasons which you either understand or don't, rates
movies by assigning numbers of cherries, with five cherries being
the pornographic equivalent of a Coppola picture, a single cherry
being so bad that one actually is made *less* excited by watching
the movie than one would otherwise have been: the pornographic
equivalent of a cold shower. The editors at *Just 18* took it upon
themselves to assign *Young Muffs 3* four cherries, when, in actuality, though not asked, I thought it deserved exactly three-and-
one-half cherries. Their explanation: Half a cherry is impossible,
graphics-wise—a claim that simply doesn't hold water. When
pressed, I am told off-the-record that there is a much deeper,
quasi-existential reason for the prohibition of a half or any other
fraction of a cherry: It is because of what the cherry supposedly
represents. Having a cherry is a black-and-white issue, rather like
being pregnant: You either are or you aren't. When I confront this
off-the-record speaker with the existential impossibility of someone having more than one, let alone *five* cherries, even if, *especially if,* one had just starred in the pornographic equivalent of
Apocalypse Now, I am called "suburban" and told to "drop it."

    All of this talk of existentialism and pseudo-philosophical

approaches to porn leads me to my second grievance: As I had many times in my brief freelance career, I selflessly, in a Christ-like gesture of choosing Truth over Profit, told the magazine that I didn't want any additional money for the additional words. Pay me for 350, get 1,500. In any other business, I would be recognized by the Chamber of Commerce and Better Business Bureau for my good works. Not so in the sticky-floored world of porn. Though I took a completely pedestrian and plebian effort (*Young Muffs 3*) and elevated it to "art" by finding deep meaning (i.e., conflict, multiple antagonists, reso-lution, Sturm und Drang, all manner of neo-Platonism, Jungian imagery and archetypes), what did they keep? The crap. When I asked for more information on the editorial policies, stan-dards, and practices over there at *Just 18*, the same off-the-record guy said frankly, "Look, the guys who read this are chronic masturbators who fantasize constantly about young girls. Even if they can read, which is doubtful, they don't *want* to read. They want to fantasize about young girls and mastur-bate. If they look at the movie reviews, they look at the titles, the number of cherries, and the stills [pictures 'captured' from the movie], and then they masturbate. End of story."

Well, tell that to Russ Meyer. Tell that to Jim Mitchell. So much for art.

But it was the third offense that was the worst, most unten-able problem I had with *Just 18:* They changed my name. First they took liberties with my cherries, then they took liberties with my prose, and now, adding unforgivable insult to injury, they had taken liberties with my name. Just *changed* it. Didn't ask, didn't consult, just fucking did it. This name-changing business gave me three specific ulcers:

1. I am a writer, despite what people say, and my byline is like gold. The more bylines I have, the more I am likely to get. In theory, anyway. Never mind that whoever directed *Young Muffs 3* didn't want credit for his work: I want credit for mine.

2. I rather like my name, but if I had to come up with an alternative, a "nom de porn" if you will, I would have come up with something cool and telling, like "Girth Brooks" or "Head Bedward" or "Oliver Secrets." What I would not have come up with, nor allowed had I been asked (which, as has been noted, I was not), was "George Gallo." I have been called a *lot* of pejorative names in my career, in my life, but never anything as cruel as goddamned *George*.

3. There is, in all likelihood, some sumbitch out there actually named George Gallo, probably the grandson of some wine magnate, who is the sort of chronic masturbator described above, who is using this glossy review in a porn rag to get elevated status in some fraternity or other.

This will not stand.

Angrily, I sat down and composed a fiery and dire e-mail:

Dear Dirt Merchants:

I take almost indescribable umbrage at the arbitrary and lame changing of my name for my review of Young Muffs 3. *I have been making my living as a full-time freelance writer for years, and I've signed my name to every dirty word I've ever written, and even a few that I didn't. But, you have deceitfully robbed me of my artistic credit, and cast shame and scorn upon my reputation. And where the hell did you come up with "George"?*

My legal counsel has advised me to inform you that I am
contemplating litigation. Vexatious, vicious litigation.

I shit on yr. Masthead,

Jayson Fucking Gallaway
(aka George Gallo because of you whoremasters)

To which they quickly replied:

Dear Fucko:

We apologize for not using your name for your review,
and we assure you we will use your actual name in any future
movie reviews we publish from you.

In a related matter, we will not be using any movie
reviews from you in the future.

If you wish to be considered for any future work, do not
ever use the word litigation in communication with us again.

Did the spelling of your name on your paycheck meet
with your approval? Please do let us know if that troubles you
at all: We can cancel it immediately.

Yrs. in escalation,
The whoremasters who pay your rent

To which I quickly replied:

Dear Sirs:

Understood. I love the checks. Please keep them coming.

Your humble servant,
George Gallo

In hindsight, I suppose the situation could have been handled
differently. Having now shot myself in the editorial foot and inad-

vertently dammed up what could have been a tsunami of free skin flicks, my only option was to try my hand (don't go there; that's my job) at this weird "set-copy" business and see what I could do.

I went back and read some examples from the two magazines they had sent me, and that, combined with my lessons regarding the masturbating simians who are this rag's demographic, led me to take a different approach. After all, any serious attempt at anything even approximating an actual female perspective for this sort of dirty work would go over about as well as that bitching-about-my-name-and-threatening-to-sue shit had at *Just 18* HQ. No female would ever write this perverted and twisted drivel. Unless, of course, she was a freelance writer in dire financial straits like me. In which case, she would write not from a female perspective, but from the perspective of what the cretinous readers of this magazine fantasized a young female's perspective would be: impossibly naïve, hornier than a Howler Monkey on Ecstasy, and alternately obsessed with and fascinated by and in dumbstruck awe of the male sexual organ. Which would not be very difficult for any writer, male or female, to do. And it shouldn't have been a tough assignment for me, but it was. I am not a pornographer, unfortunately (I've got the income to prove it). At some point, I became deluded enough to think I was some sort of *artist,* and so, even if I am writing smut, it has to have *style.*

And so it was when I put pen to paper and set doggedly at the task of composing fine filth—nymphomaniacal narratives to accompany these shoddy copies of photo layouts.

"A cool phaser-blast of ball-sap shot across her chin as she looked up into her brother's eyes and smiled naughtily."

That is just about the worst, most foul, goddamned sentence that a man can write. And I would never admit to having written it. At least not in public. Because there has to be something quite sideways and demented about the person who could even *think* of something like that. But you'd be surprised at how low one's thoughts can sink if one is getting a nickel a word. The marquis himself would have been proud.

Just as de Sade had, I learned that the key to mastering the art of composing really top-hole pornographic literature is the development of a formidable vocabulary of alternative names and euphemisms for the following things:

1. Both male and female genitalia.
2. The multifarious acts of physical congress possible between two (or three or four or 2,000 people—and, one disturbing instance in which an absurdly flexible and elephantine young man took the phrase "go fuck yourself" to a far too literal level, which has been the cause of great emotional distress and even nightmares for yrs. truly).
3. Other copulative possibilities involving a person or persons and some hapless, helpless, incongruous, inanimate object—e.g., a champagne bottle (full), a soft-drink can (in its entirety!), a baseball bat (!), a traffic cone, a piñata, a Thanksgiving Day turkey (uncooked).
4. Every actual or potential orifice in the human body, however unlikely or improbable.

As my abilities as a perverted wordsmith developed, so did my workload. Soon, I was getting assignments from half-a-dozen print magazines and online porn-movie-rental services. The movie reviews were, for the most part, fairly straightforward. I watched the movies, took copious and insightful notes, and sub-mitted my critiques. And whatever the ideographic system, be it number of cherries, number of Xs, or stages of erection of a car-toon penis, I kept my mouth shut about what the magazine or Web site chose to award the movie. As for my name, an increas-ing number of publications agreed to use my name, though each one strongly advised against it via editors who were dumb-founded and perplexed as to why any self-respecting pen would want his name associated with such putrid pornographic pot-boiler. I could offer no explanation, other than my addiction to seeing my name in print was far more powerful than any sense of shame or decency I was capable of maintaining. For a while I worked under the name Head Bedward. But, despite being one of my favorite names, it was not without substantial problems, not the least of which was that Mr. Bedward began to receive gay or otherwise male-intensive movies to review, movies with colorful titles like *Bottoms Up* and *The Man Hole* and the quasi-artsy *White Swallow*. It seems that certain assumptions are made about a guy whose first name is "Head." The spelling was changed briefly (i.e., for one review) to "HeDD," my thinking being that the big double-Ds would clue in any editor to my preference of sizable mammaries over pretty much anything male (my think-ing also being, in this instance, incorrect and tragic, resulting in yet more gay porn). I started sending letters to the good people who were sending me gay porn:

> *In these hypersensitive times, I suppose I should go on record and clearly state I have absolutely nothing against homosexu-ality. Nor do I have anything against bisexuality. Since we're on the record, I may as well mention that being a bi-woman*

gets you an automatic 20 bonus points on the Application for Girlfriend Status that must be filled out prior to any second date with me. But yes, I am completely heterosexual and male, and that means I find men (including myself) completely unappetizing sexually. Men are smelly, hairy, ungraceful, plain, and decidedly lacking in the sort of curves I find attractive. With that in mind, it should be obvious that I am completely unqualified to judge the erotic merits of any gay porn movie: The greatest gay movie ever made is just as uninteresting and unappealing to me, sexually, as the worst. I am to gay porn what the blind are to fireworks displays.

Still the flow of homoerotic cinema continued. And still the videos went unwatched (save for the onanistic thriller *Go Fuck Yourself,* where the star was able to both fellate and anally sodomize himself, which, though unstimulating and downright disturbing, I watched with awestruck fascination). The gymnastic and contortive skill involved was enviable, and, yes, despite the vehement heterosexuality discussed *supra,* I could not help contemplating the potential time, money, and stress that would be saved by having such abilities.

After a lengthy struggle for what I think was a noble cause, I capitulated and jettisoned the name and identity of Mr. Bedward. It was a cruel defeat, but in the end it was for the best. For it was only with the death of Mr. Bedward that my new porn persona could be born: Buster Hymen. *Doctor* Buster Hymen. As Buster Hymen, I churned out what arguably remains my finest filth ever, and Buster received plenty of work, all of it rewardingly heterosexual.

Despite the success I was enjoying as Dr. Hymen, cracks

began to show, not in my level of prose or ability to meet dead-
lines, but in the integrity of the adult publishing world in general. As hard as it may be to believe, it is true: The adult
industry is driven by neither the pursuit of truth nor artistic
betterment—it's all about the putrid lucre. If you want proof,
try to write a really bad review of a movie . . . not a "this is not
the best movie in the world" sort of bad review, but a "don't
waste your money on this piece of shit" sort of review. I tried.

On occasion I would write an absolutely scathing review of a
video, the sort I mentioned before that are pretty much saltpeter
for the soul. Inevitably, I'd be told to rewrite the review with a
more open mind. "Just because you aren't into something,
doesn't mean everyone else isn't." And that just pissed me off. I
always was very fair. I always gave movies a fair shake (as it
were), because yes, though it might not be my specific cup of
tease, I knew that somehow, somewhere, somebody would find
it stimulating. Even though I am not personally excited by
scenes of octogenarian women having *any* sort of sex, much less
group sex, much less *group sex with each other* (I wish I were
making this up: *87 and Still Banging!*—"These old bitches put
the 'Ass' back in 'Assisted Living!,'" "This Well-Hung Crust
Buster Is Back to Clean Out the Cobwebs in the Cornholes!"),
someone obviously is. And though amputees and cumbersomely
pregnant women with turgid tummies aren't up my alley, there
are constitutionally protected people out there who have been
waiting months for this new release, and if it was a well-done
movie about amputees, or pregnant women, or retirees, or
retired pregnant amputees, or whatever, then I'd say so.

But some of these movies were just *horrendous.* And making
bad porn is like going to prison: You have to *try.* Here's what I

mean: Anybody can fuck up once. Anyone can make an error in judgment (e.g., drinking and driving, breaking someone's jaw in an argument, shooting the neighbor's incessantly barking dog at three in the morning, etc.), and the jurisprudential result is usually not bad—probation, maybe a night in jail, and fines. You have to come back *again and again* and build up a lengthy criminal record and really *prove* to the judge that you are serious about going to prison. So it is with porn. Any jackass with a video camera, a girlfriend or two, and a case of beer can make a porno: Just drink the beer, hit RECORD, and let nature take its course. With soft-core nudity and drunken flashing being interesting enough to build a multimillion-dollar empire like Girls Gone Wild, the odds are very much in your favor that if your home movie simply shows penetration, it will be a hit. If the camera work is shitty enough, and the results look sufficiently homemade, you can market the film toward the enormous "amateur" porn-fan demographic. And if the girl or girls involved fall into any of the popular fetish genres, such as Busty, Asian, Pregnant, Amputee, Hairy, Incontinent, etc., you are almost guaranteed a huge payday. My point is that you really have to go out of your way to make something so bad that not even a prisoner with a life sentence would find it interesting. Which was the case with one particular steaming pile of sexual shit, the title of which I shall not repeat here: It was *that* bad.

So I called it like I saw it. Prisoners, institutionalized sex offenders, men who get uncontrollably aroused by used toilet tissue wouldn't even like this. At least the guy in the Go Fuck Yourself series was interesting to watch, if only from an anatomical perspective. Midget porn—same thing. But this movie offered *nothing*. The magazine refused to run the review.

Instead, they had me write copy for the ads in the back of the magazine. Oh . . . you thought those were real? Nope. I, or some freak like me, wrote them. I'm sure some porno magazines carry legitimate personal ads from women who just can't get enough sex, who want to meet men for anonymous sex, blah, blah, blah, but most are a complete setup. Here's how it works: I would write the ad. The magazine would have girls from one of their many phone-sex enterprises record messages, and then the trench coaters call the 900 number, get charged between three and five dollars *per minute,* and listen to the messages, all of which are, of course, at least two minutes long. After the message, the caller is invited to leave his information so the girl can contact him. Of course, no girl ever calls. No girl ever even hears the message. No one does. It is impossible to prove this scam, because a) not a lot of guys are in a hurry to call the Better Business Bureau about not getting any calls back from personal ads in the back of *Spankwanker* magazine, and b) if one complained, he would be told that the lady didn't find his message appealing, dismissing his legal argument and reinforcing his suspicion that he is a pitiful loser.

After a year of this, I called it quits. If you tell anyone I said this, I'll deny it, but it's true: There is such a thing as too much porn. One's threshold for shock or even arousal gets elevated to a point of diminishing returns, when you look at the pornocopia in your room and realize it ceased being cool or even clever or interesting a long time ago.

And then there's the reaction you get from the cute teller at the bank whom you've been eyeing from the line and she's been eyeing you back and then you hand her a paycheck from *Busty Bitches* or *Just 18.* It's never good.

Gossip Queen for a Day

With the Antichrist apparently still in jail, pretty much everybody cutting budgets and laying people off, and finding myself unable to deal with even writing pornography anymore, I thought I was done. What little reputation I had as a writer was, given what had been published, rather dubious if not outright dangerous. Never mind that I had written beautiful and sensitive things that showed my softer, more tender and sensitive side. It seemed that unless I put my penis in it (so to speak), nobody would publish it.

I was coming to terms with that, and getting ready to begin a new career as, I don't know, perhaps a roofer or paver of roads, when I got an e-mail from a "chick" magazine (their term, not mine) that wanted to know if I could do a little writing for them.

"Sure," I replied, reflexively. One of the first things I learned as a freelance writer is that you never turn down work. Especially not when you finished your last frozen pizza two days ago and have since been gnawing on the pizza box and other food cartons, hoping at least for a reminder of what the food tasted like.

I have no idea how this girl got my name or why she thought I could bring anything legal to a magazine created to empower and embolden a demographic that had only recently become interested in sex with boys, and was just discovering the power of the half-shirt and belly rings and pulling the sides of one's panties up from very low-cut jeans so as to be visible to the public. Either one of two things had happened:

1. The magazine had, for some time, been collecting the names of freelance writers, and had gone down this list looking for someone to take the assignment, and had received negative replies from anyone with a serious reputation or sense of self-worth. And then they got to me. Or,
2. They had done a Web search for something having to do with teen girls and writers, saw my name in the results on *Salon.com,* and just assumed . . .

Either way, they apparently were as desperate as I was, because my instantaneous, "Sure" was followed by their instantaneous, "Great, we'll fax a contract over to you right now."

I still didn't know what they wanted me to write.

As the pages oozed drearily from my fax machine, it became evident that this was no accident: This was punishment, a karmic counterstroke for my scriptorial sins. It seems I had agreed to write that most loathsome of literary forms: the Hollywood Gossip Column. Of course I wanted to back out, just pick up the phone right then and tell them to fuck off like I had that goddamn Paolo and his advance, but it was the middle of winter and conditions were getting downright inhospitable outside. This was no time to be homeless, and as my landlord would so succinctly remind me every hour when he beat on my door: "Yo rent is due, mothahfuckah!"

As I read through the contract, things just kept getting worse. My reason for blind acceptance of the job: I needed the money. Their reason for blind acceptance of me: They needed their first column by tomorrow morning.

God Himself had given me the Finger, and the heavens tittered with malicious giggles. There was no way I could do this in my regular voice. My regular voice would deliver a column that would say, "So-and-so was seen with so-and-so and who gives a shit? Fuck Hollywood." Which I don't think was the sort of column they had in mind. This would be even more difficult than writing porn. Perhaps I should assume a gay personality. Put on the Pet Shop Boys and Abba and panties some stripper had left at my apartment and hope for the best.

I can stomach neither gossip nor Hollywood—the combination of the two was far more than I could deal with while sober. On my way to the bar, I stopped at a newsstand and picked up a half-dozen of the usual suspects, or, rather, the main offenders: *The Enquirer, The Globe, The Star,* and the rest. The only thing this dark new assignment had in common with anything I had done up to this point was that I had no idea how to do it. I figured these papers would have to do for textbooks in a crash course on writing Hollywood gossip.

I put the tabloids on the counter furtively, the way "normal people" buy porn. They have their reputations to consider, and so do I. Of course, the girl behind the counter chooses this obviously sensitive moment to attempt banter.

"Just can't get enough of it, can ya?" she says with an empathetic smile.

I guffaw defensively, overachieving in my attempt to nonverbally convey the silliness and impossibility of her assumptions. This is such an embarrassing moment for me that though my words are true, I feel like my explanation is a lame lie:

"Ha ha ha . . . no, I'm a writer, and I just got hired to write a gossip column for a girl's magazine, and I don't know the *first thing* about it, and they want it *tomorrow,* so . . . heh . . . heh. . . ."

Now she is looking at me with confused accusation, like, "Dude, it's *okay,* you like what you like . . . this is San Francisco." Or something to that effect.

I fight the desire to explain more, to dig the defensive hole deeper, and just fork over damn near $30 for this library of lies.

The interaction at the bar doesn't go much better.

"That's a pile of horseshit," growls the old man five stools down. I look up from behind my copy of *The Globe.* He restates and punctuates his opinion:

"Horseshit!" he snarls again, this time pounding on the bar to cause a ripple in his Ripple. A man who is apparently Mr. Horseshit's friend, who has had his head facedown in his crossed arms on the bar, is jarred into consciousness by the pounding, and slowly lifts his head. Together these two old codgers bear a striking resemblance to Statler and Waldorf, the two crotchety old-man puppets that sat in the balcony and jeered and taunted the acts on the stage of *The Muppet Show.*

"Whaas horseshit?" slurs his friend.

"Those . . . gosship papers," says Mr. Horseshit, pointing accusingly at my tabs and me. His friend's eyes narrow as he tries to focus through an afternoon of beer. Confused and irritated, he slowly puts his head back down on his arms.

Mr. Horseshit is glaring at me as if he wants an explanation. I shrug.

"I'm supposed to write a gossip column by tomorrow, and I have no idea how to do it. I don't want to, but I have to. I need the money."

He stares at me for a few seconds as my words process slowly. Then he sighs and shakes his head. "Lemme tell ya . . ."

Oh damn. He's getting up.

"Those . . . *things* . . . they're just horseshit . . ." he blathers as he stumbles toward me. I let out a sigh myself. *Shit.*

"I can give you shum *real* goship."

"Oh?"

"Shuuuuuuuuuure . . . ," his arm is on my shoulder and his breath smells like a whole sack of assholes. I'm getting ready to break his arm when he continues. "I wuzh a famoush . . . ," he stops, apparently having lost his train of thought. But now I want him to go on. I am intrigued.

" . . . ." You can just tell it's on the tip of his pickled tongue. I'm actually leaning into him and his bitter breath in case he whispers the answer.

"ACTOR!" he roars, causing me to jump, and again awakening his companion.

"I wuzh a famoush actor in . . . ," and he is lost again. Or perhaps he just has a very bad stutter. I've heard that many actors stutter in real life, but discover that the speech impediment goes away when they are on stage, which is a big reason why they keep acting.

"HOLLYWOOD! I wuzh a famoush actor in Hollywood, and then one of these goddamn magazhhines printed bad shtories . . . LIES! And thash it . . . no more career. No more acting."

He has begun to drink my beer. This would normally be a capital offense, particularly when accompanied by the touching of my shoulder, but it's obvious he needs the beer more than I do, and I need it pretty bad.

"What's your name? Have I heard of you?" I figure since he's drinking my beer, the least he can do is answer a question or two.

"My name . . ."

Another long silence. He really is thinking . . . now would be the perfect time to take a sip of beer, but he doesn't. I briefly consider sliding the beer out of his grip and taking a belt myself, but his previous sip had been a deep one, and some of the contents of the glass had touched his ill-kempt mustache and then washed back into the glass. There were no visible floaters, but one could never be too careful.

"PAT BOONE! I'm Pat Boone."

The last time I had seen Pat Boone was about 20 years ago. Either he had aged exponentially and just let himself go all to hell, or Mr. Horseshit was full of it. I was betting on the latter when he snatched up the tabloid on the top of the pile and began jabbing his yellowed and bloated finger at the picture of Brad Pitt on the front page.

"You shee this guy . . . whashiz name?"

"Brad Pitt?"

"Dash da one Braaaaaaaad Pitt. You wan shum goship about him?"

"Sure," I said, smiling. As Pat Boone finished off my beer, I retrieved my pen from my back pocket and ordered two more beers. Pat finished the beer and then thought for several moments. I poised my pen over the last page of one of the tabloids, ready to fill the margin with gossip.

"I FUCKED HIM UP HISH ASH!"

"Really?" I asked, trying not to fall off my stool with laughter.

"Right in the ash . . . pop." I scribbled notes in the margin as Mr. Boone turned the page. I hadn't even finished the first item when he dropped a second bombshell that would rock Hollywood.

"I fucked him in the ash, too," said Mr. Boone, pointing at another picture, more calmly this time, as if reminiscing about a lost love.

"You had sex with Gary Coleman?"

"Oh yesh . . . nice boy. Very . . . nishce . . . boy."

A pitcher of beer later, I had enough scandal to shake Tinseltown to its very core. An exclusive with Pat Boone, down and out and drunk in San Francisco . . . a one-on-one interview where he admits to having sex with more than 23 prominent Hollywood figures.

I went home and wrote it up, adding a bit about Eminem being a no-talent weenie whose voice is to music what belt sanders are to nipples, and sent it off.

The next morning, the phone began ringing at 8:30.

"We can't run this!"

"Mmmm?"

"We can't run this. We'll get sued."

"Why not?"

"Oh, let's see . ... libel, slander, defamation, and that's just for starters."

"It's *gossip*."

"Yes, I know it's gossip, but we can't tell people that Pat Boone is porking Gary Coleman."

"But he said he did."

"Pat Boone."

"Yep."

"*The* Pat Boone?"

"Shit, I don't know. I don't even know if he was *a* Pat Boone. I didn't ask for his ID. . . . It's *gossip.*"

"We can't do this. All we can do is this bit at the end about Eminem. Can you add another hundred words, and we'll just go with that?"

"Sure. Gimme a couple minutes."

I don't know a thing about Eminem. I had never listened to any of his songs. I heard him on the radio, and his voice made me want to slap things. But beyond that I had no clue. And apparently, since the definition of gossip had changed recently, I couldn't say anything about him unless I had reliable quotable sources and other nonsense. So, I just wrote an indictment of rap in general, and how, though it hadn't been worth a damn since about 1992, it was permanently in the toilet with Eminem in the game now. I may have mentioned Vanilla Ice. I may have mentioned Snow. I don't remember. And I can't look it up, because in addition to the magazine getting flooded with angry letters and threats of boycotts, I personally received nearly a hundred e-mails, one agreeing with me, five death threats (!), and a virus that ate my hard drive the following week.

The magazine agreed to pay me for that column but said that would be all; thank you very much.

I was able to take a bit of solace that evening though. As bad as my day had been, it wasn't nearly as bad as the night several kids around the country were about to have.

I was able to follow up on three of the death threats that had come from kids younger than 15. I know they were younger than 15 because I looked up their return e-mail addresses, got a name, let my fingers do the walking, and made a couple of phone calls.

"Hello?"

"Hi, is Aaron there?"

"May I tell her who is calling?"

"Aaron is a her?"

"Who is this?"

"This is the gun-toting writer whose ass she promised to 'bust a cap in' and I thought I'd give her a call and talk things over."

"What?"

"Who is this?"

"This is Aaron's father."

Aaron's dad and I had a nice chat, and I called the next number. It was the most fun I've ever had on the phone sober. Adam, a young man who claimed to be a gang member with a body count, and had been stupid enough to tell me he was from Eminem's hometown of Detroit, was reduced to tears. He was 12. I don't know what happened to those kids after I got off the phone, but I suspect it was worse than being fired as a gossip columnist. Little bastards.

I Come in Peace

A friend of mine once told me, "There is nothing more depressing than hitting the STOP button on the VCR after masturbating to a porno."

He was wrong. That is merely the third most depressing thing. There actually are two things even more depressing than hitting the STOP button on the VCR after masturbating to a porno. The first runner-up is masturbating to a porno and then, at the moment of truth, having the power go out, leaving you in the silent darkness, unsatisfied to the point of anger, your dick in your hand, fumbling with your pants, stubbing toes and God knows what else, trying to find a candle or a flashlight. Now *that* is damn depressing. But it only rates second place.

Drum roll, please.

The most depressing thing in the world, the thing that is far more depressing than hitting the STOP button on the VCR postwank or having a power failure prewank, is having to aim the fertile liquid results of the abovementioned wank into a small plastic cup, maneuvering your jizz-pickle like some sort of boom on a refueling aircraft in all kinds of unromantic ways so as to catch every last drop, and then put a cap on the plastic cup, put a label on it, and write a four-digit number you've been assigned and told to memorize for occasions such as this, plus the date and number of days since your last ejaculation (not counting, of course, the one from which you are still recovering/sweating/panting/whatever). *That* is the most depressing thing in the world. At least it is to me. Yet that is exactly what I've agreed to do every Monday at eleven in the morning.

Desperate times call for desperate measures, and these have been some desperate-ass times. I have sold off all of my CDs. I've sold off most of my books. I've sponged off of everyone who has had the misfortune of sharing my last name or hanging around for more than four months without telling me to fuck off. All normal and decent resources have dried up. It is now time to sell off the only thing that has not dried up. It is time to sell bodily fluids.

Plasma is not and never will be an option. A while back, a week before undergoing a mild surgical procedure, I was asked to go to the local blood bank and give an autologous donation— a pint or two of my own blood to have on hand in case it was needed during the surgery. So down I went and, well, down I went. As soon as the nurse pricked my finger to establish what type I coursed, I turned white, went into shock, and passed out. They laid me down and said I'd have to come back again, because for some reason they could not draw the blood once I had passed out. So, I came back a few days later, got as far as the finger prick, and the room went swirling again. Eventually the doctor who was performing the surgery had to give me a couple of Valium and have me driven to the blood bank. The nurse could have cut off my entire finger and I wouldn't have minded. I have no idea how many pints she took, but I remember secretly hoping that this Valium-filled blood would be transfused during the surgery to give me a little added buzz in the recovery room.

I'd be happy to hook down a Valium or two now to go donate blood, but having no health insurance, and the price of Valium outweighing the money paid for plasma donation by about three times, it would be self-defeating, and leave me looking like a junkie running out of veins.

And I think we all know where that leaves us.

The ad had run in the back of the San Francisco independent papers every week for years, but I had never even thought about actually reading it. Now I am ripping through the papers trying to find it. Here it is:

SPERM DONORS—GIVING TO A WORTHY CAUSE NEVER FELT SO GOOD!

Get paid for something you're already doing (and help build families). The Sperm Bank is looking for healthy men of all ethnicities to become paid sperm donors. To be eligible, you need to be:

- **Between the ages of 18 and 40.**
- **Able to make weekly visits to our downtown office during business hours.**
- **Able to make a one-year commitment.**
- **Able to provide general information about your biological family's health history.**

Hmmm. Well, I am a chronic masturbator; I am within the age limits; I have no plans during business hours for this or any other week in the foreseeable future; and I have no reason to expect that to change in the next year. Never mind that horseshit about helping to build families: I just want to know what the payday is for this gig. I pick up the phone.

During the first ring, it occurs to me that perhaps I should have thought about this a bit more before dialing. By the second ring, I decide that this is an exceedingly bad idea and I should hang up immediately. Just as I move the phone from my ear, someone answers.

"Sperm bank."

Click. I hang up.

Shit. What am I thinking? Am I so desperate that I am willing to go to some office in the Financial District and masturbate into a cup? At that moment, my stomach emits a 13-second operatic gurgle that sounds rather like a kitten trying to squeeze into a garden hose. *Yes, I am desperate.* And who knows? Maybe there is no plastic cup involved in the equation. Maybe I've got completely erroneous notions about sperm banks. Perhaps the 21st century has seen bold innovations in reproductive technologies, with the development of special machines, or even particularly talented people, to extract the needed substance from its source. How bad can it be? No worse than the Happy Booths in the backs of the adult bookstores that I've frequented during particularly dark chapters of my past. *Fuck it.* I hit REDIAL.

"Sperm bank." The voice is female and sultry. Smoky. I guess maybe I had hoped not to talk to someone sexy.

"Um . . . yeah . . . hi. I was interested in becoming a donor."

"Great. What's your name?" This woman actually purrs as she talks. A highly unlikely mental picture is forming: I'm imagining Catherine Zeta-Jones in black lingerie sensually caressing the "receiver" (the one on the telephone and the other one) as she asks me questions about sex and my sperm.

Approximate Transcript of Telephone Conversation Between Sperm-Bank Employee (at Time of Conversation Thought to Be Catherine Zeta-Jones in Lingerie) and Jayson Gallaway (Masturbator for Profit):

Jayson: My name is Jayson Gallaway.

Catherine: And your address?

Jayson: 4540 California Street.

Catherine: And how did you hear about our donor program?

Jayson: Actually, I've seen your ads in papers for years, and times are tough, so I thought I'd give it a whack. I mean . . . I thought I'd check it out.

Catherine: Do you or any member of your family have a history of mental illness?

Jayson [caught off guard and lying]: No. Hell no. We are all *perfectly* sane.

Catherine: Have you ever had sexual contact with a prostitute or any other type of sex worker?

Jayson: Why else would you hang around them?

Catherine: So you have had sexual contact with sex workers?

Jayson: Well, not *all* of them. I'm very selective. Is that a bad thing?

Catherine: Do you have any sexually transmitted diseases?

Jayson: No. Absolutely not. No nothing. Not ever. No STDs, and perfectly sane. That's me.

* * *

It goes on like this for another few minutes, with questions about general health and surgical history and so on. I imagine Catherine with the board game Chutes and Ladders in front of her: Each question I answer correctly, I get to move up another square. Totally sane: Climb a ladder. Fuck a hooker: Down a chute. After this battery of questions, she apparently concludes that I qualify to move up a significant ladder toward the prize: the title of Sperm Donor. She would like to schedule an initial appointment, a personal consultation. Her description of that is very frank, the sort of frankness I am not at all used to from total strangers, except in emergency rooms and 12-step programs. She is either a seasoned veteran or she is reading from some sort of script:

This consultation will take about 15 or 20 minutes. We'll have you fill out some forms and a detailed questionnaire. Then, I'll discuss some of the legal and ethical aspects of sperm donation in general, and in the state of California in particular. There is a six-to-eight-week screening period before you are approved as a donor. You'll need to abstain from ejaculating for 48 hours before each appointment. You provide samples by masturbating in a private room. During the screening, we evaluate your fertility, test you for sexually transmitted diseases (you'll be asked to provide blood, urine, and semen samples), ask you to complete an extended family history form, and send you to our doctor for an exam. If you are approved as a donor, you're paid $50 for each ejaculate (visit) that meets our minimum sperm count—this includes retroactive pay for the sample you've provided during screening. Sound good?

She read the entire thing in less than 10 seconds, so the only part of her spermatic soliloquy that I had actually heard was the part about 50 bucks per pop. And that was enough.

"Sounds great."

"Terrific. Right now, our schedule is pretty open. Can you come in tomorrow? Will that work? When was your last ejaculation?"

Jesus, Catherine . . . what ever happened to "What's your sign?"

The truth is that it's been about 17 minutes since my last ejaculation, and I was rather looking forward to another in the next hour or so.

"Tomorrow's out. What else have you got?"

"Let's see . . . tomorrow's Friday . . . how about Monday?"

That would be fine except I have a sex-worker girlfriend who looks forward to frequent and forceful sex on the weekends the way Somalis look forward to the arrival of food trucks at UN distribution centers, and she has been known to react just as, if not *more,* violently than they do if unsated.

"Um, hmmm . . . Monday doesn't really work either. How about Wednesday . . . Wednesday morning?"

"Eleven-thirty okay?"

"Perfect."

"Okay then, we'll see you at eleven-thirty next Wednesday morning. Do you know how to get here?"

She gives me directions, telling me the building is next door to a large hot-dog stand with a huge hot dog on the roof that you can't miss. I bust out laughing, failing to quell the uprising tidal wave of adolescent, smart-ass-yet-really-unavoidable potential remarks. What was on the other side of the old fertility clinic? A bunny farm?

The weekend is predictably and atavistically carnal. As my sex-worker girfriend is sorely limping around, getting ready for work on Monday morning, I tell her about the whole sperm-donation thing and the requisite 48-hour period of abstinence required of donors. She is not happy, but is less not happy about not getting any than she is about the profound lack of money around this crap hut lately. There is no spoken conclusion, so I just assume I have her support and cooperation on this.

Ha.

That very evening, this girl, a staunch vegetarian, is cooking a heavily marinated tri-tip on the smokeless indoor grill wearing—I shit you not—a thong and a half-shirt that says "Got Milk" across the boobs.

The next morning, as I'm dialing the sperm bank to change my appointment to Thursday, I realize that this is not going to work. There is simply no way that I am ever going to last a full 48 hours living with a nymphomaniac who has perhaps the most extensive collection of lingerie and thigh-high pleather boots in existence, which, like the preponderance of her footwear, were not designed with bipedal locomotion being a serious consideration. I guess 24 hours is pushing things, but it will have to do. Forty-eight hours is just a recommendation . . . a guideline established by average people with average sperm.

My sperm is not average: I just know it. Twenty-four hours is ample. More than enough. I don't make the call.

The sperm bank is within walking distance of my apartment. I try to stroll calmly, but I feel like I'm wearing a sandwich board exclaiming "Will Wank for Food."

Within minutes, I see the hot-dog stand, with its huge decorative bunned weenie on its roof, offering a 12-foot visual clue as to the establishment's board of fare, as if the enormous red neon HOT DOGS sign is not enough.

My palms begin to sweat, the dark irony of which would cause me to laugh or at least smile under normal circumstances. But I'm beginning to understand that there are no longer "normal circumstances" in my life, ever. Which, I guess, logically, makes this a normal circumstance, so I laugh. I am getting ready to go into some monolithic office building I've never seen before, talk to some total stranger about my sperm, and then whack off into a cup. Given the year I've had, this is just another day at the office. Besides, how many times have I gone into equally unfamiliar buildings in far worse neighborhoods and asked some tattooed felon behind the Counter for a handful of tokens, then, clutching my fistful of tokens, gone wandering into some dank, dark, murky, often downright threatening labyrinth of tiny video-preview booths, and done the exact same thing *sans* cup? But even though one can hardly call those places "romantic," this place is just so . . . professional looking. No tanning neon. No one loitering spookily. It's just so . . . clinical.

Just as I'm thinking I might walk on by and forget the

whole ridiculous deal, a voice in my head speaks up: *Fifty bucks per squirt.*

It takes an awkward few seconds of scrolling through the electronic directory of business names next to the dial pad and speaker at the entrance of the building that houses the Semen Savings and Loan. On the first floor next to the front door, separate from the rest of the interior offices and open to the general public, is a deli. Behind the counter is a lethargic and bored Korean girl in her late teens or early twenties staring at me the way only fresh immigrants stare at people in America. Your average American citizen will put up with about seven seconds of solid stare before either winking or throwing a punch, because other Americans know that to stare at somebody for more than five seconds means *something*. But maybe it's not because she's new to this society. Maybe she knows that I am just another pathetic float in the daily parade of wankers who show up here in 15-minute intervals to spank for the bank. Yes, she *has* to know. I *know* she knows. With the monopoly on quick lunches that the large-weenied hot-dog stand next door has, she makes maybe three sandwiches during her lunch rush, and spends the rest of her shift watching pathetic and swarthy morons show up and mutter something into the speaker, enter, and reappear 5 or 10 minutes later, panting slightly, clothes ever-so-slightly disarranged from when they entered, reaching for and lighting and savoring with subtle satisfaction a long draw from a Camel. She knows. Everyone knows. I am here to masturbate. And I am here to do it for cash.

"Hello?" crackles the voice over the speaker. I have the instinctual need to order a hamburger and large fries.

"Um . . . this is Jayson."

Bzzzzzzzzzzzt.

Upon entering, one has no choice but to go up the stairs. I remember at some point in my phone conversation with Miss Zeta-Jones that the spank dump is on the third floor. So far, everything, the walls, the stairs, the floor, everything, is that horrible shade of institutional blue. This is far and away the least sexy environment I have been in all week. *Shit. I've been to churches that are sexier than this.* Even the deli downstairs with its catatonic clerk and her accusing glare is more alluring than this place.

At the third floor, there is a formidable metal door (also institutional fucking blue) with a button on the wall next to it. Above the button is a handwritten note covered in Scotch tape: "Press Button for Entrance."

I am a bit daunted at just how well guarded this sperm is. Why is that? Does sperm have significant black-market value? The floors of the aforementioned private-viewing booths are literally coated with the stuff, and they have to pay hapless illegals with no English skills subminimum wages to don opera-length rubber gloves (thick enough to handle weapons-grade plutonium) to mop it up. No . . . I can't imagine any masked gangs in paramilitary gear with guns storming the sperm bank and demanding jizz. So why this Pentagon-like security? Perhaps the porn in the private collection rooms is so lurid, like government-issue porn, that perverts everywhere would go to great lengths to have at the stash. I dismiss this idea instantly, but will soon have the notion proved wrong for me.

My palms are now sweating profusely. My finger almost slips off the button when I press it. Another brutal buzz. A bolt clicks as I push yet another door open. I feel like I am arriving for an audience with Hannibal Lecter.

No more blue, thank God. Now it's just cold, sterile, impossible-to-hide-or-even-be-subtle-in white.

Catherine Zeta-Jones looks much different in person than she does on the phone. Her coloring is similar, but that's about it. In real life, she is short and squat, maybe 20 pounds overweight, a probable lesbian, and answers to the name of Karen. At least that's what her name tag says. Karen is very pleasant and welcoming, but has a certain indefinable edge that only a woman who has worked in a sperm bank for a couple of years could have.

Karen invites me to sit in her "office," which I honestly think was intended to be a broom closet or some random storage space. Karen actually has done some nice decorating here, starting with a coat of pleasant, decidedly uninstitutional rose.

In her office, Karen asks me a few more medical questions: nothing terribly interesting or intrusive. When she mentions needing blood, urine, and semen samples, I'm tempted to act out the punch line to an old joke and just hand her my underwear. But I decide against it. As you sadly know (see "Great Italian Magazine Swindle," and ibid.), I don't wear underwear. My answers seem to be the right ones, and I feel like I am simply flying up the ladders toward my Pulling for Profit victory. But then she drops the bomb: In addition to the already absurd and unrealistic expectation that I abstain from sexual healing a minimum of 48 hours prior to my visits, she now is telling me that I am not supposed to smoke marijuana.

"You are not supposed to smoke marijuana," she is telling me. I look at her as if she's just told me I'm going to be the Grand Marshal of this year's Gay Pride Parade, and I will be required to don a studded leather thong and a sash that says "Ass Kitten" while smiling and waving from a 30-foot float of a giant lubricated anus.

I suppose some explanation is in order here. See, the last few months have been what is usually described in contemporary urban patois as "a bitch." Nothing has gone right. I have been fired from jobs and replaced by lobotomized felons because they had, and I quote, "better work ethics and standards." I only wish I was kidding. On the grand scale of employability, my rank is officially somewhere beneath people who literally have to sign out of halfway houses and take drool-inducing medication before they can leave their residences for work. I am in possession of a perfectly valid master's degree and the only potential income on my ever-darkening horizon will depend on my ability to squirt enough viable spermatozoa into a Dixie cup. This is my reality and has been my reality for months. And I am so deep in debt that even if I am found to be a viable donor, it will take some sort of personal bukakke tsunami to cum up with the kind of cash I need to extricate myself from this seemingly endless paralysis of poverty. Sobriety is not an option, drinking costs and causes unpleasant hangovers, and around here, pot is free. And now this . . . this . . . sure-to-be lesbian is asking me to endure not only 48 hours of orgasmic abstinence and organic sobriety, but also telling me that I have to do this for 8 to 10 weeks, and then, *maybe* I'll get paid? And that payment is stipulated on my agreement to maintain such behavior for the next year?

"Marijuana lowers the sperm count," she says.

I'm still looking at her as if I'm perched on the Giant Anus Float.

"Are you out of your fucking tree?" I say in an unfortunate moment of pure reality.

Karen seems shocked—or at least a bit taken aback. She shuffles the papers she had been using to take notes nervously. "Is that a problem? You said you were not addicted to any substance."

I look at her squarely. "And so I am not. I am not *addicted* to anything. But I'm in the middle of a pretty difficult time in my life. Things haven't been working out too well. That's pretty much why I'm here. And I'll be honest with you, Karen, without weed and wanking, there is not a whole lot to my existence these days."

She looks nonplussed. An army of thousands of picketers and protestors have shown up in my brain and are chanting things like: "Whaddawewant? WEED! Whendawewannit? NOW!" and holding banners that say: *No Wank, No Weed, NO WAY!!!*

But then that same damn voice taps my psyche on the shoulder, whispering its mantralike reminder: "Fifty bucks per squirt." Considering that in all likelihood, if I give Karen the Finger and walk out of here right now, I'm just going to go back to the crap hut and jack off anyway, what the hell?

"Okay," I lie. "No weed."

"Great," says Karen, relieved, but still in a bit of shock. "It really does reduce your sperm count."

Not *my* sperm count, by Christ, I think to myself. That myth was no doubt the product of the same wrongheaded virgins who established that 48-hour bullshit. *I'll show these hippies what sperm really is. Give me the goddamn cup. Better yet, give me two . . . I might blow the bottom out of the first one.*

But we're not there yet. Apparently there is one more ladder to climb. Karen's voice, which has been completely clinical up to this point, now turns oddly personal. It's jarring, the way an R&B singer who's just finished blazing through "Brick House" lowers his voice and brings the microphone closer to his mouth and says, "We wanna slow it down a little bit right now." And you just want to scream at him (as I often do when drunk at wedding receptions): *"Fuck you . . . don't quit now . . . you had a groove going. Rock on, you funky motherfucker! C'mon! Tear the roof off the sucker . . . turn this mothah out! Sing it, bitch!"*

But no. Just when I'm ready to double-cup it, Karen wants to slow it down.

"I want to speak with you about our donor identity-consent program . . ." and goes into an unintentionally semi-patronizing tone usually only heard in commercials for tampons or yeast-infection medications. Basically, she wants me to sign this consent agreement that says that any hale issue resulting from my contributions to the cup can, upon their majority (which is their 18th birthday in California), get my identity, track me down, and ring my doorbell all day, claiming to be the fruit of my looms. This concept vexes me intensely. Eighteen years from now, I'll be, like, 50 fucking years old. I have no idea if I'll even have a pulse at that point. And if I am still above room temperature, *who knows* what I could be doing? About the only thing I am damn sure of at this point is that if the next 18 years are anything like the first 30 were (and let's face it, the odds are good: the die has been cast), the *last* thing I could possibly need is some pimple-ridden adolescent who just got the vote darkening my door and claiming that he or she is family. I'm not all that crazy about the family members that I know about, much less any postpubescent freaks wanting money for college or, more likely, bail money and legal fees. No. Fuck that.

Still, Karen is hopefully enthusiastic and persuasive, and this is obviously something she has elected to make a sort of personal crusade, this obtaining of permission for strangers to go knocking on the doors of other strangers from whose testicles the former stranger had supposedly sprung.

"This sounds like something that can be decided later, no? After all, we don't even know if I'm a 'viable donor' yet." (I have intentionally neglected to tell Karen about my Super Sperm hypothesis. Superior genes are no reason to go cutting in line. I shall endure the tedious hoop-jumping that these other, lesser-seeded mortals require, if only to keep up appearances and not seem arrogant.)

Karen seems to sense my thoughts, for suddenly, almost magically, she produces a small, sealed, clear plastic bag containing an equally clear plastic cup and a plastic lid (not so clear) for the plastic cup.

All right—showtime!

"So, this is the container we use for our sample collection . . ." Karen tears open the bag and arranges the contents of the bag on her desk. She explains the purpose and/or function of each item. As she does so, for reasons I'd rather not explore the psychogenesis of, I feel like a police-academy cadet being taught how to use a rape kit. Perhaps it's just the awkwardness and self-consciousness and, let's face it, embarrassment that anyone with any sense of coolness must feel in such a situation. I suddenly understand why so many women abhor the idea of male OB-GYNs.

"So, what we're going to do is have you go into one of our

'collection rooms' and obtain a sample, which you will collect in this cup."

I give Karen about 15 Bonus Points for constructing that delicate sentence about as perfectly as possible, avoiding crude and gruesome terms such as "masturbate" and "ejaculate" that, while totally fine in a medical sense, would not have kept me in the calm and surprisingly relaxed state of mind I'm in, bizarre surroundings and sweaty palms be damned. She continues.

"As soon as you have your sample, use this lid to cover the sample immediately," and she places the cover on the cup. This demonstration of something so obvious reminds me of the insipid perma-grinning flight attendants who show what one can only assume are cretins how to buckle and tighten a seatbelt. Minus two points for Karen, but I'm still with her.

"Then you take this label and write your donor number . . . oh . . . we didn't give you a donor number yet." She punches a couple of keys on her computer keyboard and jots down a four-digit number on what is apparently becoming my "file." She writes the same number on a business card for me to keep. "This is your donor number. This number is how we'll identify you from now on, so whenever you call or come in, just use this number . . . you'll never have to say your name."

I feel a tad insulted. What's wrong with my name? I guess some people have privacy issues. But once I'm up here, behind the multiple security doors and whatnot, I'm okay with things. It's just the approach to the building and that damn Korean sandwichmaker and her knowing stare that give me the Creeps. But whatever. Donor number it is.

"So, you'll write your donor number, the date, and the number of hours since your last ejaculation. And then, this is *important*: Put the sticker on the side of the *cup, not* the lid. It looks like it should go on the lid, but we don't care about the lid . . . we care about what's in *here.*" She thrusts the cup forward at me for punctuation. I nod my understanding, but my mind already has moved on to what's next. These "collection rooms" sound rather spooky and euphemistic. What will they be like?

"Do you have any questions?" Karen is good. She is genuinely concerned. I shrug. Despite all of this pro forma spermatic stultiloquence about consent laws and motility and permissions and viability and weed and where the fucking sticker goes, I'm just here to jerk off into a cup and cash a check. *C'mon, Karen . . . let's get this party started.*

"Oh . . . a couple more things . . ."

Fuck! Come on!

". . . in the rooms are some tubes of lube . . . if you need lube, please use what's in there . . . don't bring your own . . . other lubes will taint the sample."

The fact that the word "taint" has entered into this conversation in *any* context is cause for more involuntary laughter. Actually, it's more of a nose-based chortle. Karen gives me a look that tells me she doesn't get it. "Taint," it seems, will never be part of the urbane lesbian vernacular.

There are four "collection rooms." Unoccupied rooms' doors are left open, and a green light glows above the door. All necessary supplies will be found in the amply stocked rooms, so one may come empty-handed (again, as it were). I am told to close and *lock* the door as soon as I enter. Locking the door will activate the red light above the door. It also activates a red light on an esoteric control panel just above the light switch inside of

the room, on what is soon to be my side of the locked door.
Karen's final instruction to me is that when I am "done," I am to
press another button on this same control panel, and then wait
for the red light on my control panel to turn green. She empha-
sizes the extreme importance that I stay locked inside this room
until the light turns green. *"Why?"* I ask. She explains to me it
is simply to keep the various donors from running into each
other in the hall or at the counter where the samples are
handed over. Initially, this strikes me as silly and frivolous. But
upon further consideration, I can appreciate the potential awkwardness of two guys bumping into each other, or just hanging
out at the counter, each with that postorgasmic aura, known in
some circles as the "Hi-Pro Glo," each clutching a plastic shot
glass full of semen. What the hell would you say to each other?
You'd have to say *something*: The tension of the silence would
be unbearable. It would be the awkwardness that a guy feels
when another guy sits right next to him at a bar. At least there
you can talk about football or something. No dice here. Two
guys lean up against the counter at the sperm bank, holding
their samples like beers: "Nice load," says one to the other. No.
Fuck that. That is all wrong. Karen is right. I shall remain
ensconced until I get the Green Light.

She asks me again if I have any questions, and once again I
shrug in the negative. "Okay then, you're all set," she says, and
nods almost imperceptibly, like a mother encouraging her bash-
ful child into the classroom on the first day of school.

I close the door. I lock the door. I lock the *shit* outta that
door. The lock is the basic button-you-push-in-and-it-stays-in-
until-you-turn-the-knob-from-the-inside kind of lock that is
ubiquitous in American office bathrooms. Not only do I push

the lock in, but I *really* push the lock in. I *lean* on the motherfucker. Just to be sure, I turn the knob to see that the button
pops out again. I crack the door slightly, push the button again,
and try to turn the knob from the outside. It is *locked*. Karen or
one of her assistants is probably watching this comedy from
somewhere, but I couldn't care less. I need utter confidence in
the security of this room if I am to truly focus on the business
at hand (once again, as it were). I close the door, lean and lean
and lean on the lock until I am sure beyond any doubt that no
one is getting in here without a battering ram and a search warrant. Feeling I have achieved privacy, I relax a bit and turn
around to survey my surroundings and get comfortable.

I'm not sure what I expected, but this ain't it.

The room is reasonably spacious, given its limited purpose:
It is roughly the size of an economy cabin on a cruise ship. The
room is a few degrees below what I would consider "room temperature," though I suspect that this is by design given what
occurs here. The floor is black-and-white tile and looks like an
oblique chess board: a *cold* oblique chess board. What takes up
most of the real estate in the room, and what is most genuinely
surprising to me, is the presence of a bed. Yes . . . an actual single bed, with the whole works covered in that weird pale green
paper that is omnipresent in hospitals and assorted medical
facilities everywhere. The presence of the bed is surprising to
me mostly because of the laws of gravity and other inescapable
laws of physics that are simply not at all conducive to filling the
cup. Given that the goal here is to collect a *liquid* sample in a
small plastic cup, and given the notorious lack of directional
control males have over any liquid emitted from the snotty end
of their joy sticks, it would seem to me exponentially more dif-

ficult to capture much of a specimen of anything whilst horizontal. I am somehow reminded of the carnival games on the midway at the State Fair, where one tries to pitch a dime onto a relatively horizontal surface (typically an ashtray with a Mötley Crüe or Budweiser logo on it) and the unlikelihood of success in such endeavors. Are there men who can lie horizontally and shoot so high that they have time to grab the cup and maneuver it into position to collect a sufficient sample on its plunge back toward the earth? I don't know. I've seen my share of porn, God knows, but I've never viewed it from such a strategic, physically tactical perspective. And the whole notion of this bed being here solely for the purpose of men to lie on it while masturbating gives me the sort of sexual creeps that typically land people in therapy. No. I shall not lie on this bed. I shall stand. I am a vertical masturbator. Always have been . . . always will be. And I shall stand in the spot in the room where I estimate the fewest number of men have stood.

There is signage on fluorescent-colored sheets of paper with bold black print placed all over the room, which don't so much kindly *remind* as they do nastily *hammer* donors with the various prohibitions, warnings, and recommendations that Karen has given me. The signs are ominously and potentially disturbingly laminated in protective, easy-to-clean plastic. As is the case with about 95 percent of my life, I really can't believe I'm here, now, doing this. I take a deep breath, think of the money, and resolve to do my duty: This is for the Cause.

Near the bed, as promised, is a large basketful of the plastic packets containing the cups and labels. I pull one out and open it just as Karen had done. When I go to throw the plastic wrapper away, I see several other such wrappers, along with all manner of other tissues and sanitary wipes and latex gloves and God only knows what all else in the wastebasket. For reasons not even worth exploring, this depresses me. Okay . . . perhaps "depresses" is the wrong term. But whatever sights there are that induce libidinous thoughts and the urge to orgasm in me, this is the opposite thereof.

There is a sink where I lay out these receptacle materials, and obeying the fluorescent orange laminated sign to "Please wash my hands with soap," I do.

I suppose the most egregiously incongruous element of this glorified jack shack has got to be the 6-by-15 foot uncurtained and unblinded and unshuttered window. Granted, the window looks out onto a brick wall about 10 feet away. But it's not just a window. It's a *really big* window, by any standard. I mean, if you were looking at apartments and walked into the living room and saw this window, you'd say, "Jesus, that's a big fuckin' window." The landlord would probably use it as a selling point and justification for an additional 100 bucks on the monthly rent. But I'm not shopping for apartments. I'm getting ready to masturbate here, for fuck's sake, and I'd prefer to do so in a room that didn't have a window the size of Montana in it. And sure, granted, it faces a brick wall, but if you try, if you get close enough, from certain angles, you *can* see things—other windows and such—and thus, if I stand right up there next to the window, I assume I can be seen. And any hapless or knowingly horny office worker taking a smoke break up on the roof has a straight shot into this horrid little room. The only safe place for this is going to have to be back over there in front of the sink, with the goldfish bowl full of packets of lube and the requisite mirror one finds over sinks in bathrooms. This is bad. I don't think I have any outstanding self-image problems, but I'm not even close to the level of narcissism required to become sexually aroused by looking at myself in the mirror.

It is then that I notice the small, two-tiered, black plastic rack affixed to the wall. There are four or five magazines in each tier, and I find out the hard way (for lack of a better term) that the bottom tier (of course) contains exclusively homosexual material, while the rags on the top are for the heterosexually oriented. The selection proves to be lame. Three issues of *Playboy* and a *Penthouse*, each of which is at least two years old. Two *hard* years (and not the good kind of hard). They are worn. I decide right then if any pages, even *appear* to stick together, I am leaving.

I don't know if this is true of most people, maybe I've been rather spoiled, but personally, I find dated porn erotically null and void. Subconsciously, even consciously, I need to know that the women at whom I am looking still at least resemble their appearance in whatever magazine or video I currently am examining. Otherwise, somehow, on some weird psychological level, it is fake to me: nothing more than a picture, as boring as photos in some stranger's old photo album, the only difference being the lack of clothing and presence of exotic locales and illogical footwear. This selection sucks. Not even a *Hustler*. No *Swank*. No *Juggs*.

I am suddenly keenly aware of the passage of time: How long have I been in here? Are they keeping track of my time out there? If I stay in here too long, will they knock? Check on me to see if everything is okay? This is horrible. I want to go home. I want to smoke pot and watch *Jerry Springer* and feel relatively better about my life, which has become so pathetic that I find myself . . . here.

Fifty bucks per squirt . . . fifty bucks per . . .

With time ticking away, I grab a couple of the magazines, put them on the basin of the sink, and start flipping. And yes, some of the pages do seem to stick together a bit more than one would expect from those in a glossy magazine. But I can't leave now. That would admit defeat. I am sure Karen and her minions are out there watching the clock and hastily organizing some slapdash office pool with bets being placed on how long I will take. The person whose guess is the closest to the time when I finally press the button to signal that I'm "done" wins the whole pot of money. The person furthest from the time of splashdown has to collect and examine my little pot of sperm. I'll bet even that Korean meatmonger is down there wondering when I will again appear in the doorway to the building, lightly glazed with sweat, looking an ounce lighter, and just a tad less tense than I did when I entered. These are the things going through my head as I flip sticky pages searching fervently for arousal. There is nothing. These magazines are weak, and, for my money, barely qualify as actual porn. I think that perhaps I should bring my laptop with me for my next visit—the content of the smut collection on that very hard drive would make these paltry pages seem like the *Highlights* magazines found in pediatricians' offices. I'll have to ask Karen about that one. What I *should* do is bring Miss Ain't-No-Way-I'm-Going-48-Hours-Without down here with me to lend a proverbial hand. But considering Karen and crew are so militantly against even imported lube, I strongly doubt some chick in hot pants and platform heels would ever even be let into this building. They'd make her sit down there with that Korean sandwich slinger while I was up on the third floor handling business (and yet again, as it were).

Still flipping pages. *Christ, this is ridiculous*. Evidently, people really *do* read *Playboy* for the articles, because there are more arousing photo spreads in *National Geographic*. My thoughts wander back to the Korean girl downstairs. Despite her laserlike glare, she might look okay naked. At least that's what I'm imagining right now. . . .

Oh for fuck's sake! This is pathetic. There is no way my imagined game of hide the pastrami in Miss Korea's buns can outdo *Playboy* and *Penthouse* in the erotic department.

The flipping of pages is growing desperately audible, and I'm sure Karen et al., can hear me in here, searching for acceptable stimulation, probably wishing to Christ that I'd just find *something* and bring things to a climax so they can go to lunch. And what about Karen? Catherine Zeta-Jones she ain't, but right now I can use all of the help I can get, and if sperm donation really is as important to her as she makes it out to be, surely she'd be willing to give a brother a squeeze. Lend a helping hand. Regrettably, in addition to her probable lesbianness, she strikes me as the sort of woman who spends her evenings training in vicious martial arts and has no time for impoverished freaks looking for free hand jobs.

And then, it happens. I've said it before and I'll say it again: Salvation does indeed have many faces, and today, two of those faces belong to Belinda Carlisle of the Go-Gos and '80s one-hit-wonder Tiffany. Each are featured in different issues of *Playboy*, and, though 15 years too late (in my opinion), better late than never. And better late than never is rapidly becoming my personal motto for what is turning out to be a far more arduous ordeal than the simple crank-spank I had anticipated. And so it is, just like in real life, that I find I must choose between two women: They are on completely different pages in completely different magazines, and there's only room for one magazine on the basin of the sink. And I can't deal with any more flipping of pages. After all, I need some sort of manual dexterity with an opposable thumb. Tiffany is looking pretty damn good, but the pages of the Tiffany layout seem to be much more "adherent" to each other than the Belinda Carlisle section. It seems obvious that Belinda has been saved for me. She has been waiting for me. So Belinda it is. If God had even the slightest shred of pity for me, His humble servant, He'd have graced these pages not with a Go-Go, but with Joan Jett. Ah . . . Joan. My little heartthrob since 1982. *I Love Rock and Roll* was one sticky album cover, as I recall. I wonder if Joan is straight? Who cares. How about me and Joan tying up Belinda, demanding proof that her lips are, in fact, sealed . . . showing her who's *really* got the Beat. Oh yeah . . .

A few minutes later, my sample is capped and labeled. My handwriting on the label is blatantly shaky. I imagine they get a lot of that here. One second you are in the throes of autoerotic rapture, and the next second you are fumbling stupidly with a goddamn cap and trying to scrawl information on a tiny label. Imagine it: There you are, eyes rolled back in your head, you and Joan Jett are riding Belinda Carlisle like a sexy seesaw, a big-tittied teeter-totter, and not a breath later, you've got to focus and aim at and within the narrow circumference of a Tupperware shot glass.

I fold up Belinda, replace her on the hetero shelf, and look in the mirror. It is manifest that I have achieved dramatic, albeit self-induced, sexual climax within the last minute or two. The glaze of nervous sweat that formed as I approached this building is now beaded and dripping lightly. My face and neck are flushed. My respiratory rate is visibly increased. My clothes are disheveled. I wash my face and try to rearrange my clothes properly. But why? Who am I supposed to be fooling? There is simply no escaping the fact that when the stupid light turns green, I'm walking out of here clutching a baby-food-sized jar containing semen with my name scribbled on it in a jerky postorgasmic script next to the date and the utterly bunk prior spank time of 44 hours. So let's quit the charade: I just jacked off into a cup and the staff of this whole freakish place knows it.

I still feel a bit hot and winded and sweaty and disheveled and well, now . . . a bit . . . unprolific. As I've said, these cups are somewhere between a shot glass and a baby-food jar, sizewise, and my output has been . . . well . . . not nearly as voluminous as I would have liked, and not nearly the half-pints I've seen shot across many a TV screen by X-rated movie stars. Hmmm. I scratch out the "44 hours" bullshit and replace it with "27 hours." Didn't bother to mention that in the same period I smoked enough ganja to fuel an entire reggae band for a world tour. But there is no getting around it: My love-lava flow is suffering. The cup doesn't runneth over; it runneth decidedly under.

To make matters worse, Karen has evidently given up waiting for my slow ass and has gone out to lunch. She left in her place a blonde cutie with gorgeous eyes and a sweater the tightness of which is the sort that causes traffic accidents. She smiles. I hold a jar of jizz. She takes it and looks at it curiously. *Shit.* She's looking at how paltry an amount there is. It's probably not even enough to prove anything in court. In fact, it's probably not even enough to affect the taste of a cup of strong coffee. But it's mine, dammit. This is *my* seed, the label says so. She smiles and thanks me as if it was just revealed that I was her Secret Santa at the office Christmas party and I had gotten her a snow globe (filled with sperm). She purrs something about freezing and testing, and could I give them a call tomorrow, please? All I want to do is leave, which I do. The place is much easier to exit than to penetrate (as it . . . oh, never mind). Miss Korea looks like she hasn't moved at all and her gaze is just as intense as before, with perhaps just a hint of smile the likes of which are usually seen on the lips of people who are comfortably on the inside of an inside joke.

The next day, after a night of pot-fueled sex, I call the sperm bank. I tell them my donor number and remind them that they asked me to call today. I wish it would have taken more time to look up my file and check the results of their testing, but the girl on the phone (who is not Karen and I suspect is the hottie with the sweater) knows exactly who I am and knows the exact results of the test off the top of her head, as if the whole damn office has been talking about this all day. "Well . . . we didn't have enough sample to freeze. Can you come in and give another sample?"

I almost drop the phone. *How the hell can there not be enough to freeze?* You can freeze a drop of water, ferchrissake . . . they call it "snow." And while I admit it had not been Viagra Falls, I know it was more than a fucking *drop!* I saw it. *I* could have frozen it. Give me a toothpick and an ice-cube tray and I could have made them a spermsicle.

All right, fine. Day after tomorrow. No sex. No giving in to G-strung cookers of steaks. No porn. But I'll be damned if I'm putting away this bong. Fuck you and your 50 bucks, Karen. You ain't the boss of me.

Somehow, some way, I give them not only 48 hours, but an overachieving 53 wretched, horrible, wasted hours of sexual abstinence.

I was in a very dark mood indeed when I rounded the corner and saw the weenie stand and its skyscraping sperm-sucking neighbor. No sweaty palms this time. And as soon as I feel that freakish Korean's glare burning into the back of my skull, I turn around, look at her sharply, and slowly lick my lips with outright aggression, perhaps sexual, perhaps with more psychotic intent. Her face crinkles unnaturally and she turns away and begins slicing meat—cathartically, I suspect. I pound the buttons on the dial pad like they owe me money, and rather than mumbling my four-digit number like some mincing little man-bitch in County Jail, I speak like MacArthur: "I am here to deposit."

Bzzzzzzzt.

The buzz comes a little quicker than it did the last time I was here, but not as quick as I will once I get upstairs. I march up the nauseating aquamarine stairway and lean on the second button like my *Three Stooges* nightmare when Moe administers a lethal poke to Curly's eye after he's just found out Curly's been diddling his daughter in the two-hole. I shove open the formidable door and barge into the office like a man looking for a recepticle. Again it is the tight-sweatered tease behind the desk. She senses danger . . . menace . . . aggression. I suspect she can actually see the semen that has backed up in my system, all the way to my eyes, giving them and me a downright demonic look.

"B is open," she says, pointing to the open, inviting door of the second collection room. In I go.

This room is different than the room I was in before. Same sort of uninviting bed, same sink and mirror. This basket is more full of plastic cups than my previous room, and that's a good thing. I haven't gone more than 48 hours without an orgasm since I was seven years old. They may need to hose this room down once I'm through. I pull three plastic cups out and arrange them carefully on the sink's basin like a bartender preparing to pour shots of tequila for a pack of party girls before a wet t-shirt contest. Nary a drop shall be spilt!

And oh look, an entirely different selection of magazines. *Whoops* . . . not really. Same article-intensive publications, same two-tiered sexual preference. But at least it won't be another self-inflicted nut bust based on a woman whose anthem centered on the notion of sealed lips. Forget *Playboy* . . . they've become nothing more than *Ranger Rick* for grown-ups. *Ah-ha!* A *Hustler*. Now we're talking. And bingo . . . I open right to a spread (yep, a spread) of an amateur-looking bachelor party. It is darkly lit, and these girls look real. Things are looking up. Things are, in fact, pointing up as I turn the page to see how the bachelor party progresses. But before I can focus my full attention on this carnal soiree, something else catches my eye. It is a small black box on a small white table, about knee-high. *Am I being recorded?* Before I can proceed, I must investigate this black box.

It is a device that . . . well, makes fake noise. Background noise. There are about five settings to choose from: all quasi-natural "white noise." There is "Ocean," there is "Creek," there is "Rainstorm." And there is the seemingly meteorologically improbable "Soft Thunder." Hmmm. I've never seen such a machine, nor known of a commercial need for such a device. Is this something that Radio Shack provides to sperm banks the way the Gideons stock hotels with free bibles? I am fascinated to the point of distraction, and to distract me from the page in the pictorial where the girls begin wrestling in a kiddie-pool full of cherry Jell-O takes a lot.

I press the ON switch and am immediately blown back by the deafening roar of what is supposed to be a "creek." Fucking thing sounds like a ballistic missile strike. Apparently, the previous occupant of this pecker-paste production pen had a sense of humor on the level of the high schoolers who loosen the caps on the salt shakers (or maybe it was that bitch Karen; I had her pegged as a man hater from the beginning). Now that the entire building has been startled by the scream of a digital creek, I lunge at the box. There is no easily identifiable volume control, so I start beating the thing against the wall. The resulting pounding noise is no doubt as audible as the Screeching Creek of the Apocalypse, but I'm losing my hearing with each passing second. After about seven solid blows, the machine seems to remember its place on the food chain and submits. The digital Rainstorm begins at soothing, relaxing levels. Especially in light of the thrashing it has just received, it actually does sound like rain. I like rain. I like the sound of rain on windows, on the roof. But unless it's a real downpour, it usually doesn't instigate any sexual mood for me. In reality, after a few seconds of Rainstorm, I have to pee. And, of course, there is no toilet in here. And now, thanks to the Rainstorm, that inescapable threshold has been crossed where there will be no sexual arousal until micturation.

Christ.

I press the button to indicate I'm "done" (the world of sperm donation is black and white: there is no button for "I'm having unforeseen audio and urinary problems in here").

The light immediately turns green. I open the door and am greeted by the incredulous stares of sperm staffers who are really not sure what to make of the digital sibilant din and barbaric pounding that has been coming from collection room B. They look intimidated.

"Where's the bathroom?" I demand. No one says a word. Karen points west. I take a step in that direction and she pipes up: "You should shut that door so no one else goes in there." I do.

A few minutes later, I return to collection room B to find it unchanged, undisturbed: The mouths of my three cups hungrily awaiting my seed. I close the door, perform my paranoid/obsessive four-check-locking ritual (worth noting here that such checks occur *nowhere* else, not when I'm locking the car, not the apartment—just here at Karen's House of Jizz). I'm still confused and somewhat daunted by the presence of the bed. Given the reputation men have for falling asleep after sex (and it's not our faults, girls—science shows that orgasms release a sedative chemical in our brain that encourages, if not induces, sleep [ironically, an opposite stimulant is released in the female brain, causing them to want to talk and cuddle and such. It's true. I read it somewhere]), what if you come in for your spank, and you're a bit stressed and traumatized because you've been agonizing through 48 hours of white-knuckled, teeth-gritting frustration, and you lie down on this weird bed and get all comfortable, drop trou, manually agitate, erupt, collect, and then stereotypically roll over and doze? Is Karen or one of her reproductively ripe right hands going to knock inquisitively? Do they have a passkey? They must. The existential likeliness of a passkey nullifies my thoroughness in the lock department and causes my testicles to retreat almost completely into my torso. *Those fuckers have keys.* But maybe they don't. Then what? Call the authorities? San Francisco's Finest kicking in the door, or those fuckers at SFFD with their goddamn bolt cutters hook-and-laddering up to this huge window to find some freak with his pants at half-mast, in a clammy post-ejaculatory nap barely balancing a brand new batch of baby batter on his belly . . . such scenes should not be running through my fragile psyche right now. What happened to the pictures of the strippers at the bachelor party? Ah yes . . . here we are. *Focus.* Nice. The one in the white thigh-high boots looks enough like my ex-gf on a really good day to cause unexpectedly quick arousal. I wonder whatever happened to her. I wonder what she is doing right now. I know what I'd *like* for her to be doing right now. Yes. Brace yourself, plastic cups . . . this is the moment you've been training for.

Mere seconds away from what I'm predicting will be a flash flood of fluid, I see it: a pube. Not my pube. A foreign pube. *Fucking A!* My mind scrambles back to the ex in the thigh-high boots and sets them in motion . . . straddling me for the lap-dance of a lifetime . . . but resistance is futile. There is simply no denying the foul and horrific presence of some dude's pube here, on the basin of this supposedly hypersterile environment. I feel as if it is looking at me. *Taunting* me. "Fuck you," the pube seems to say. I would rather have encountered a live cock-roach than some shitbag's errant pubic hair. Whatever "mood" I had managed to achieve in these sterile and dire settings is gone. Over. The credits are rolling.

But surrender is not an option. I mean *really*. I don't believe there is a language in the world that has a word that accurately describes the sort of loser who can't even get sexually interested in himself. I mean, sure, rejection from outside parties is a stan-dard feature of the sexual landscape of every hetero guy. But to emerge from a collection room in a sperm bank empty-handed (so to speak) is simply untenable. What possible excuse could there be? Whenever your hand falls asleep during onanistic sex, it is seriously time to consider the priesthood.

To my ultimate shame, and in an act that is as close to gay as I will ever get, I actually lean down and blow this foreign hair clear. At first, it doesn't budge, and I have to blow harder. Then it blows back against the mirror and is carried on the breeze back in the direction of my face. I want to use one of the receptacles to capture the hair and have a DNA test done and find the identity of the pantload that grew and inconsiderately shed this short-and-curly, and I want to hunt him down and set him ablaze. I wish him ill in extremis. I at least want to plant one of my intimate bits in some disturbing and personal place in *his* world. Like his toothbrush. Fucker.

So finally the pube is gone, but I know it is still here, still near, watching me. Back to the bachelor party, where the girl who looks so pleasantly like my ex is doing some sort of erotic per-formance art involving cherries, chocolate syrup, and a daunting amount of whipped cream on the torso of one of the other strip-pers. Nice. Very nice. I bet I know where that cherry's going . . .

But before I can turn the page to find out, a loud, resonant, bassy, testosterone-fueled moan comes from the room next door. A second or so later, another, less exuberant, but just as mood-killing moan follows. This guy has just filled his cup, and the whole goddamn floor heard about it. He has no shame, this professional masturbator whose climaxes are evidently so grand as to elicit involuntary and spontaneous compositions of arousal-apex arias. The sounds are really more Gregorian Chantish than they are operatic. But who the fuck cares? Between the pube and the moan, I'm much closer to vomiting than I am to ejaculating.

In desperation, I return to the little black box I had brutalized only moments ago. I am tender, almost apologetic as I restore it to its original upright position. Not anxious for another trip to the bathroom, and having vowed not to leave this room without a cup of cum, I select the only non-water-intensive sound there is: Quiet Thunder. It is Too Quiet Thunder: It is Silent Thunder. I turn up the volume a bit in hopes of sonically blocking any more moans or strange disturbances from the world outside this room. This might have worked a while ago, before I beat the tar out of the little black box, but after my wrath, the fragile and sensitive piece of technology is a bit out of whack. Pressing the Quiet Thunder button now causes the thing to emit loud, squawking fart sounds at 10-to-15-second intervals. The variable time intervals, coupled with abuse-damage variance in the digital recording that was once intended to sound like Quiet Thunder now makes the whole thing sound like Loud Flatulence. Given my recent hurried trip to the bathroom, and now these digitally emitted gaseous explosions, the girls behind the counter must certainly be drawing dark conclusions about the occupant of collection room B. The STOP button has been rendered useless during the pounding, so I finally just unplug this insipid machine. I must not surrender. *I will prevail.*

I grab a new magazine from the hetero tier and lie down on the bed. Fuck it.

Surprisingly, the bed is quite comfortable in spite of the sterile green quilted paper that covers both bed and pillow. That it is "pillow" and not "pillows" is significant to me. I mean, here I am, horizontal, on my back, trousers at half-mast, trying to manage a plastic cup (I have given up on the idea of the ejaculate hat trick—I'll be lucky, given the way things are going, to put even one to good use). So trying to manage one cup, and then, due to the pube and the moan, my imagination is too polluted and preoccupied to be a reliable source of erotic fantasy material, so a magazine is necessary. Without being too graphic or gruesome, I will say simply that I am right-handed. Given that what I'm here to do will be occupying my right hand completely, you can imagine the physical and logistical hurdles presented by attempts to manipulate both receptive cup and skin mag and, well, skin.

Pause here for a moment as I do, and imagine being on the set of a porn shoot, with, like, three surgically perfected sex goddesses in bed with you, surrounded by all manner of camera crew, sound engineers, directors, and miscellaneous adult industry factota, and having all of these people expecting penile gallantry at unnatural angles for the camera's benefit and so on. *Christ!* And here I am, alone, in a room with my hand and a cup and no one to please but myself and I am failing shamefully at even that. How do they do it?

Wait a minute . . . let's get back to that idea of me on the set

with the three porn chicks: Talented young ladies whose physical attributes and abilities are the finest money can buy. *Yeah . . .*
there we go. In my mind, the director and all others have disap-
peared, and now it is just us: Me and these three ladies who are
so good at sex they get paid well to perform it, and there is no
bullshitty script, and the title of the film is *What Cums Natu-*
rally and okay, the magazine slips off the bed, quickly forgotten,
leaving me with the cup in one hand, Little Elvis in the other,
and my head swimming with improbable positions and carnal
acts that some states still have legislation against, and . . .

And my fucking cell phone rings. Loudly. I can hear snickers,
actual snickers coming from the women that staff this evil goddamn place. The phone continues to ring, and it's not just ringing . . . nooooo . . . it's playing "Ode to Joy." *Fuck you, Ludwig.*

The phone is just out of reach, being in my left pants
pocket, which pocket is now around midcalf level. I literally
drop everything, prop myself up, grab desperately at this beep-
ing boner blocker.

"What, goddamnit!?"

"Are you okay? Why do you sound so upset?"

It is my mother.

I am speechless. Angry at God for doing this to me. A
buzzing begins in my head like what I imagine Ted Bundy or
Jeff Dahmer heard just before a kill. The buzzing fades slowly
and is replaced by John Lennon singing, "nobody told me
there'd be days like these."

"Hi, Mom . . . kind of in the middle of things right now."

And without warning, I realize I have officially hit Bottom. It
just doesn't get any worse than this. Nothing, not even a proctol-
ogist with depth-perception problems, is more uncomfortable

than a phone call from mom whilst midstroke at the sperm bank.

"What are you doing, Jayson?"

"I'm, uh . . . working on my car . . . I've got oil all over the place . . ." Which is not entirely untrue, except for the car part. "Can I call you back later?"

"Sure, honey . . . what time?"

Fuck's sake. And I know those evil lesbians are out there, cackling at my what-must-be-hard time, or unhard time, or whatever.

"Seven. I'll call you back at seven, Mom."

"Okay, Jayson, and don't forget I love you."

"I love you, too, Mom."

"Okay . . . be a good boy, and God bless."

I surrender. I quit.

There is a mechanism, some psychological on-and-off switch that automatically and with great force eliminates the possibility of any sort of sexual interest, arousal, or fulfillment, for at least one half hour after hearing your mother tell you to be a good boy and that she loves you and God bless you. There may or may not be any scientific evidence to back this up, but take it from me: It is fucking true.

Shamefaced, I confess to a notably unsurprised Karen that I'm having some difficulty obtaining a sample due to circumstances beyond my control, and could I perhaps come back in an hour or so? Karen, showing an apparently sincere understanding, proves me wrong in my assumptions of mockery from the staff . . . or at least from her. She says, "Of course," and even pats me on the back. I don't have the guts to ask if this has ever happened to anyone before, because I'm afraid that I pretty much know the answer.

As encouraging as Karen continues to be, my mood is damn foul. Just before I get to the ground floor, I decide that if that goddamn sandwich pimp looks at me with so much as a *hint* of smirk or sneer, I will set her on fire.

The doors open to reveal the deli counter unmanned. Unwomanned. UnKoreaned.

There's the huge hot-dog stand, with its eternally erect symbol protruding forth. In the same amount of time that I've been wasting up there on the third floor, this hot-dog monger has probably made $75, maybe more, and not suffered nearly the stress and humiliation that I have. And I *still* haven't seen a dime. I don't even know if I ever will.

And then, *She* walks by. No . . . "walks" is the wrong verb. She *bounces* by. Well-worn combat boots up to perfect knees where black fishnets over red tights take over and climb up into a miniskirt, not too tight but tight enough, and a tight red t-shirt housing things so perfect that for an instant I believe I have proved the existence of perpetual motion. Normally, my eyes would never make it further north, but it is well worth the effort, for here is a girl that looks, for my dark intents and purposes, a lot like Fairuza Balk, walking a huge dog with not a leash but a *chain,* with dark and unsubtle makeup, a nice number of very complimentary piercings, and an extremely complex dual-mohawk that would be ill-advised on pretty much anyone else, but on her it is fucking *perfect,* and I stand there as long as I can before my interest becomes conspicuously visible.

Yes, at that moment I could have dialed the code into the security dial pad with something other than my index finger, but I don't. Not right now. Anything touches Little E and it's getting soaked.

"Hello?"

"It's me."

That's all I have to say. They know. The door buzzes and is slammed out of the way. As I climb the stairs, I pry my cell phone from my now strained pants and turn it as off as it can be turned. I even disconnect the battery.

The door opens to reveal Karen holding the security door open for me. Smiling, she knows nothing needs to be said. And the look in my eyes assures her and all others that anything impeding my way is in grave danger of being mounted and impregnated. Directly into collection room B. I lock the door once without double-checking it. No bed. No fake rain. No shitty pornography. Just give me the fucking cup and stand clear.

Exactly 47 seconds later, I want a cigarette. I don't even smoke, but *damn!* If ever a cigarette was called for, it is now. Which, upon brief reflection, is about as pathetic a commentary on my life as anyone can come up with. And still, in my glorious autoerotic glow, I am disappointed in the results. Putting on the cap and filling out the label, I dunno. I mean, I guess it's okay. There is tangible *weight* in the cup. But it's certainly not the stuff porn careers are built on. And certainly not reflective of the what-I-consider-to-be-Herculean effort that went into obtaining this cocktail.

I reassemble myself quickly and hit the post-sample-attainment "I'd Really Like to Leave Now" button. The light comes on red.

And it stays red.

Fuck. Still red.

I'm getting a bit irritated. Part of me is sincerely considering running after Little Miss Dangerous, intercepting her daily canine ambulation, and laying what would certainly be the most original, albeit warped, pick-up line/introduction on her: "Um . . . hi . . . excuse me . . . yeah, hi . . . my name is Jayson and well, this is just going to sound weird as hell, but I was standing back there, in front of the sperm bank and the Weenie Hut, frustrated at my inability to arouse myself to the point of climax due to foreign pubes and digital farts and my mom calling and stuff, and yeah, but so anyway, I was standing out there wondering just what the hell to do when you came boun . . . er . . . walking by, and pretty much solved my problems for me, and like three minutes later, I was blowing baby batter into a plastic cup, all thanks to you. So yeah, you wanna go out for a drink or dinner or something?"

Finally, after a frustrating eternity, the red light turns green. I hand over my sample to Karen, who is almost glowing with pride. But not glowing the way I am. She tells me to call in a day or two, and I leave. Quickly. Hit the street and go south, her last known direction.

A bit out of breath to begin with, I never do catch up to Her. And that is probably for the best. It is probably specifically for freaks like me that the huge chained man-eating quadruped is maintained. Alas. Another dream dashed on the rocks of reality.

Speaking of dashed dreams, I called the sperm bank the next day, and Karen, with perfect professional frankness, tells me that while my sperm count is fine, and actually a bit on the high side (a-ha! I knew it! Super Sperm!), and I'll have no problem having children, the inconsistency of the volume of my output makes me ineligible to be a donor.

I'm not mad at Karen, but I do take umbrage. How inescapably, undeniably lame is the man who can't even make a buck as a sperm donor? A rhetorical question, sure, but one that is worth answering.

But I'm okay with that. I long ago came to terms with my essential lameness. It just means I have plenty of room for improvement and growth. All that's needed, I think, is the right person to grow with. All I need is Her. So, if you are a well-endowed punk/goth girl fitting the description *supra* who was/is prone to walking her dog on a chain in San Francisco, I'd love to hear from you. I'll meet you by the huge weenie in the sky and buy you a hot dog. Or a sandwich from the deli around the corner, even though the chick that works there gives me the creeps.

And don't worry . . . tell your dog I come in peace.

Acknowledgments

While I really do acknowledge the tireless support, inspiration, and exhaustive work done by my penis for this book, I would be completely remiss in not acknowledging the help of some truly great and talented people. They encouraged me, helped me, bailed me out, hooked me up, and sometimes even saved my life, and they must be thanked.

Mom and Dad—God only knows how they resisted drowning me at birth, putting me up for adoption, et cetera, but somehow they persevered, put up with more crap than any two people who ever undertook parenthood should ever have to deal with, and not only do they still talk to me, but they even invite me over for major holidays and accept collect calls. They are my makers, and I owe them everything.

Mary and her family—Rarely is a person lucky enough to have one great family . . . I have been given two. They have been welcoming, supportive, loving, and just incredible as they've watched me grow from the little pain-in-the-ass I was coming out of high school to the absolute bastard I've grown up to be. Mary is my soul partner . . . a left brain to my right and a right brain to my left. Twice in my life I have woken up in an ICU, and both times she has been there. Enough said, but enough could never be said. Thank you, and I love you.

Jenny Bent, my agent—The Velvet Hammer. Thank you so much for your support and belief. I owe you a career.

Luke Dempsey, my editor—This book would be a lesser thing without your guidance. Thanks for rolling the dice.

Big Thanks also to: Kris Larson, Shannon Haire, Robert Pimm, Doug Cruickshank, GettingIt.com, Gruner und Jahr/Momdadori, James Matranga, Anbolyn, Terri Nunn, Tim Warren, Marc Bertonasco, Olivia Castellano, Ken Kesey, Jeff Schwamberger, and Corinne Asturias.

Extra-special thanks to the Wallaces for housing me so I could finish writing this book. My laptop would never have worked in the rain.